THE CLOUD OF UNKNOWING

PARACLETE ESSENTIALS

THE CLOUD OF UNKNOWING

Foreword by Robert Benson

CONTEMPORARY ENGLISH VERSION
BY BERNARD BANGLEY

PARACLETE PRESS
BREWSTER, MASSACHUSETTS

The Cloud of Unknowing

2006 First Printing
2009 First Printing This Edition
2010 Second Printing This Edition

ISBN 978-1-55725-669-0

Library of Congress Cataloging-in-Publication Data

Bangley, Bernard, 1935-
  The cloud of unknowing / edited and modernized by Bernard
Bangley.
      p. cm. — (Paraclete Essentials edition)
  Originally published: Brewster, Mass. : Paraclete Press, c2006.
With new foreword.
  ISBN 978-1-55725-669-0
  1. Mysticism. I. Title.
  BV5082.3.B36 2009
  248.2'2—dc22

                                    2009021178

10 9 8 7 6 5 4 3

Published by Paraclete Press
Brewster, Massachusetts
www.paracletepress.com
Printed in the United States of America.

CONTENTS

FOREWORD

As the anonymous writer of the letter to the Hebrews reminds us, we are indeed surrounded by a great cloud of witnesses. One of them is another unknown writer, the one who wrote this little book that you hold in your hands.

The writer was a part of that great river of christian prayer that has been offered down through the centuries, prayed by thousands upon thousands of saints, both known and unknown, sustaining the life of the church itself. It is a great river of prayer that we are called to join when we hear the call to pray without ceasing. It is a great river of prayer that is made up of different streams of prayer, different ways to pray.

We moderns tend to make our prayers verbally for the most part. These days more and more of us practice the tradition of the daily office, the saying of collects in our worship services, and the praying of the psalms in the same settings. Extemporaneous conversational prayer, both public and private—"our ongoing dialogue with Christ," as Brother Roger of Taizé called it—has long been a part of prayer practice for most of us.

The Cloud of Unknowing offers us a glimpse into another way of prayer, contemplative prayer. It is prayer that is centered around listening rather than speaking, being rather than doing, searching for God's presence rather than searching for answers or blessings or mercies. It is a way of prayer that has deep roots in the Christian tradition and yet has not been commonly practiced by us moderns.

The anonymous author offers straightforward talk about the joys and the obstacles, the consolations and the doubts, the practicalities and the possibilities that are a part of this way of prayer. He also offers us way of infusing our actions in the world with light that comes from contemplative prayer.

"When there is a crisis in the Church," writes Carlo Carretto, "it is always here: a crisis of contemplation."

In the noise and the rush of the modern world in which we live, our need for contemplative prayer is increased, not decreased. Our unknowing of this way of prayer does not diminish its importance.

The unknown writer, one of the unknown saints, part of that great cloud of witnesses, invites you to join in this way of prayer.

And so do I.

—*Robert Benson*

INTRODUCTION

I f you are serious about your prayer life, this book is for you. The writer offers helpful spiritual instruction for those who are learning to pray, guiding them logically and clearly toward ideal prayer—what he calls "perfect" prayer. This anonymous fourteenth-century author of *The Cloud of Unknowing* originally prepared this book for cloistered English monks. A keen observer of human behavior, he laughed down the violations of good common sense that he saw religious communities employing.

Though scholars have struggled for centuries to discover the writer's identity and to place him in a particular religious order, the humble guide stubbornly remains unknown.

He is not interested in telling us how profound his own prayer life is, though we can clearly see that it is substantial. Instead, his intent is to extend a helping hand to the rest of us. He communicates, as Jesus did in the Gospels, with ordinary, everyday language. No doubt he would have been astonished to discover how many would find his little book a key spiritual guide down through the centuries.

In his time, England and much of Europe were immersed in mystical religions. Practitioners of necromancy and sorcery experimented widely. The whole culture was intensely religious. Into this context Christian mystics, addressing the devout life, introduced a healthier spiritual tone and wrote what were to become timeless works. Meister Eckhart, Henry Suso, John Tauler, Walter Hilton, Julian of Norwich, Richard Rolle, Catherine of Siena, Thomas à Kempis, and others wrote during this period.

The fourteenth century was also a time of social, artistic, and political revolution. The unknown writer of *The Cloud* gives that century and following centuries something genuine, something worth our aspiration. He does so with a smile on his face and a twinkle in his eye. He is attractive to readers in the way that Jesus Christ is attractive: He is serious without being stuffy. He talks about important religious issues, but he does so without becoming haughty.

The anonymous author is intelligent, but he avoids and criticizes convoluted academic style. A master of hyperbole, he employs colorful language to emphasize the spiritual hazards of formal education. He does not come across as anti-intellectual, but simply observes that theological erudition offers little service to one's prayer life. What we find in these pages is a healthy mysticism simply based in growing toward God. It is not a book of spiritual tricks that lead to a quick jolt of spiritual fireworks, but offer little for the remaining journey.

The Cloud of Unknowing contains seventy-five chapters (*chapitres*). For such a slim book, that equals about one chapter per page. While they may seem more like section breaks than new chapters, they are markers along the way of sustained and developing thought. Although he briefly digresses a time or two, he otherwise sticks tenaciously to his subject, and at the end of the book he returns the reader to the place he began.

The author sometimes struggles to express himself clearly, fearing that his readers will only take his words at face value. He knows that, if readers do not keep in mind the overall direction of the book, they may wind up in seemingly contradictory theological dead ends. For example, when the writer mentions that the idea of God, being spirit, is more compatible with a purely spiritual desire (one not based on emotional human desires), some may read that and come to an erroneous conclusion. Rather than leading the reader into a trap, he points out that the purer our spirituality, the more it is in harmony with God's spirit.

Some modern readers may have difficulty with the concept of the devil, or Satan, who is often mentioned in *The Cloud of Unknowing*. The author attributes many religious mistakes to the devil's work. I have included these passages as the author originally expressed them. As you read these sections, remind yourself that religious thought in this period of our history includes the active influence of a personal devil. In Wartburg Castle, where Martin Luther worked on his translation of the Bible, tourists are shown a spot on the wall where Luther threw an inkbottle at the devil in 1521. His hymn, "A Mighty Fortress Is Our God," assures us that devils, who threaten to undo us, fill our world:

> *For still our ancient foe*
> *Doth seek to work us woe;*
> *His craft and power are great;*
> *And, armed with cruel hate,*
> *On earth is not his equal.*

Thomas Aquinas, in *Summa Theologiae*, writing in the thirteenth century, points out that Holy Scripture describes the properties of intelligible things with natural images. Following Aquinas, the anonymous author contends that angels and demons can take on the bodily appearance congruent with the content of their business among us.

As you read *The Cloud*, you may detect the influences of other writers. Thomas Aquinas and Anselm were certainly on his bookshelf, but many other authors also influenced him. In chapter 35, the author recommends an unnamed book, likely *Ladder* by Guigo II, as it contains the same four devotional steps he discusses in *The Cloud*: reading, reflecting, praying, and contemplation. The writer mentions other unnamed books, but likely refers to Hilton's *Scale of Perfection* and Denis's *Mystical Theology*, from which the closing chapters gain their tone.

When I read two modern versions of *The Cloud of Unknowing* back in 1983, I kept my red "reading pencil" busy, underlining and commenting to myself in the margins. As a matter of interest, I pulled these books from my shelf to see what I had done. Curiously, the red marks diminish sharply at chapter 62 and do not pick up again until chapter 68. The book's character changes dramatically in this passage. Where the author has been spiritually arcane, he now becomes philosophically abstract, following the writings of St. Augustine regarding the dynamics of human consciousness. In *De Trinitate*, Augustine distinguishes between *ratio superior* and *ratio inferior*. Our unknown author incorporates these valuable ideas into his work, and I have attempted to retain the distinctly different style and tone of these sections.

Repetition of ideas is characteristic of the classical writing style of the period. While this may help to drive a point into memory, it seems like wheel-spinning to modern readers. Our anonymous author avoids this hazard. *The Cloud of Unknowing*, already a brief book, does not cry out for condensation, as do other spiritual classics. I omitted only a few repetitious sentences and paragraphs in this modernized version.

I am not attempting to present the definitive edition of *The Cloud of Unknowing*. Our generation already has several good ones. Instead, my desire has been to prepare a clean, smooth, easily read modernization that avoids antique syntax while remaining faithful to the teaching of the original. I do not attempt to explain ideas with my own amended comments. What is esoteric in the original remains esoteric in this version.

A comparison of texts demonstrates the uniqueness of this book.

ORIGINAL TEXT

Goostly freende in God, thou schalt wel understonde that I fynde, in my boistous beholdyng, foure degrees and fourmes of Cristen mens levyng; and ben theese: Comoun, Special, Singuler, and Parfite. Thre of theese mow be bigonnen and eendid in this liif; and the ferthe may bi grace be bigonnen here, bot it schal ever laste with outen eende in the blis of heven.

MODERN ENGLISH EDITION BY JOHN WATKINS

Ghostly friend in God, thou shalt well understand that I find, in my boisterous beholding, four degrees and forms of Christian men's living: and they be these, Common, Special, Singular, and Perfect. Three of these may be begun and ended in this life; and the fourth may by grace be begun here, but it shall ever last without end in the bliss of Heaven.

THIS VERSION

My spiritual friend in God, this book is an attempt to pass along to you some important lessons learned from experience.

There are four degrees of Christian living: *ordinary, extraordinary, unique,* and *ideal.* We can experience the first three in this life, but the fourth is heavenly. Yet by the grace of God, we may begin the ideal here and see it continue for all eternity.

HERE BYGYNNITH
A BOOK OF CONTEMPLACYON,
THE WHICHE IS CLEPYD
THE CLOWDE OF UNKNOWYNG,
IN WHICHE A SOULE IS ONYD WITH GOD.

Here begins a book of contemplation,
which is called The Cloud of Unknowing,
in which a soul is united with God.

PRAYER

O God, all hearts are open to you.
You perceive my desire.
Nothing is hidden from you.
Purify the thoughts of my heart
with the gift of your Spirit, that I may love you with a
perfect love and give you the praise you deserve.
Amen.

PREFACE

In the name of the Father, the Son, and the Holy Spirit.

Here is a message for the unidentified person who is holding this book. Whether you own it or have borrowed it, whether you are taking it to someone else or intend to read it yourself, please respect the special nature of its contents. This book is for devout followers of Christ. Those who have not already learned to pray and who desire a life in service to Christ should read it. If such a person does read this book, or hear it read aloud, it may not make any sense. Therefore, when you read it, be sure to read the entire book. As the text develops, you will find that a question you had on an earlier page will find an answer on a later page. To read only a section means that you will be taking a passage out of context, and this could be misleading.

I do not intend this book for everyone. I do not want clever clerics and self-appointed critics discussing it. I would prefer they never see it. I did not write this book for them and do not want them involved with it. I prepared this book for souls inclined to contemplative prayer. Perhaps, by God's grace, this book may be a helpful source of guidance.

My book contains seventy-five sections arranged in progressive order. By the time you read and ponder all of them, the final section will help you determine if you are being directed toward contemplative prayer.

THE CLOUD OF UNKNOWING

CHAPTER 1
Four degrees of Christian living

My spiritual friend in God, this book is an attempt to pass along to you some important lessons learned from experience.

There are four degrees of Christian living: *ordinary, extraordinary, unique*, and *ideal*. We can experience the first three in this life, but the fourth is heavenly. Yet by the grace of God, we may begin the ideal here and see it continue for all eternity. I list these four degrees as stages in ascending order. If you make progress through these stages, the merciful Lord has called you and is leading you to himself by these same degrees.

Early in your life, you lived in an ordinary manner with your worldly friends. The everlasting love of God created and redeemed you. God also inspired your desire for him. It was as though God attached to you a leash of longing and led you to himself. God brought you to the place where you can be a servant among his special servants. You have an opportunity now to discover a deeper spirituality. New possibilities await you.

Consider your own life. Notice God's love drawing you carefully, almost imperceptibly, to the unique third degree of the Christian life. You stand on a steppingstone, the starting place of the road to ideal spirituality. You may begin living on this level now, *before* you die, as well as for eternity.

CHAPTER 2
Spiritual preparation

Take a good look at yourself. Who are you? What makes you worthy of your call from God? (Probably, God is now disturbing the sleep of a lazy person.) Never forget your spiritual vulnerability. God's invitation into a unique relationship does not make you better or holier than others. Instead of feeling proud of yourself, exercise humility. Christ emptied himself of equality with God when he was born in human form, humbling himself even to the point of death on a cross.

Now Christ has graciously selected you from his large flock of sheep to be one of his special followers. He brought you to this place of pasture that you may graze on his love. This kingdom of heaven is your heritage, and God asks you to claim it.

Do not hesitate to make that claim. Forget the past and press on to the future. Remember your spiritual needs rather than your spiritual achievements. If you want to progress to the ideal, you must hunger for it. Strong desire must direct your will. It will become yours by the power of God and with your consent.

Let me remind you that God loves you as a jealous lover loves. The distraction of other desires interferes with your progress. God accomplishes this work in you only in privacy. He wants to be your only love. Look toward God and let him act beyond your ability. Your job is to keep the windows and doors of your soul open, but screened against insects and vermin. If you will do this, your humble prayer will be attractive to God. Call upon God and notice his warm response. God waits for your cooperation.

You ask, "How do I continue? What shall I do next?"

CHAPTER 3

A superior discipline

Let modest love prompt you to lift up your heart to God. Seek only God. Think of nothing else other than God. Keep your mind free of other thoughts. Give no attention to the things of this world.

These pages describe spiritual contemplation that is pleasing to God. When the saints and angels observe you in this state, they rush to help you. Devils will be disturbed when you begin, and they will use all their tricks to discourage you. In a mysterious way, your contemplation of God helps others even as it helps you.

Contemplation is not difficult or complex. Enthusiastic desire will accomplish much. With God's gift of spiritual hunger, you will make steady progress. Continue until your prayer life becomes enjoyable.

When you begin, you will experience a darkness, a *cloud of unknowing*. You cannot interpret this darkness. You will only comprehend a basic reaching out toward God. None of your efforts will remove the cloud that obscures God from your understanding. Darkness will remain between you and the love of God. You will feel nothing.

Accept this dark cloud. Learn to live with it, but keep looking, praying, and crying out to the one you love. Any insight you ever gain of God while you live in this world will be in this cloud and in this darkness. If you will continue in the manner I describe, I believe that God, in his good pleasure, will grant you an instant of profound religious experience.

CHAPTER 4

Knowledge and imagination

I do not want you to have misconceptions regarding the contemplative work of the soul. Therefore, let me describe in detail what I have learned about this plain and simple practice.

Many think contemplative prayer takes a long time to achieve. On the contrary, results may be instantaneous. Only an atom of time, as we perceive it, may pass. In this fraction of a second, something profoundly significant happens. You only need a tiny scrap of time to move toward God. This brief moment produces the stirring that embodies the greatest work of your soul. How many desires can fill an hour? You may have as many desires as there are indivisible fractions of time in an hour.

If you were as sinless as Adam was before the fall, you would be in total control of each instant. You would respond to every divine impulse. Everything about you would reach toward God all the time, because God created us in his image. In the Incarnation, Christ emptied himself, becoming one of us, accommodating himself to our limitations. Only God satisfies our spiritual hunger. Nothing else suffices. After God graciously transforms our soul, we begin perceiving what is ordinarily beyond our comprehension. Angels don't have the mental capacity, nor do we, to grasp the total reality of God, but what cannot be ours by intelligence can be ours as we embrace love.

Every rational creature has both the power of knowing and the power of loving. Our Creator endows us with both, but

God will forever remain incomprehensible to the knowing power. Through loving power, however, each of us may know God. Love is everlastingly miraculous. May God help you to understand what I mean, because endless joy waits for you.

If God were to bless you with absolute control of your will, you would have a constant awareness of heavenly bliss. My enthusiasm should not surprise you. God designed us for this. God created us to love, and everything else in God's creation helps you love. The exercise explained in this book will restore our spiritual consciousness, but if we neglect prayerful contemplation, we sink ever deeper into unawareness.

Pay attention, then, to how you spend your time. You have nothing more precious than time. In one tiny moment of time, heaven may be gained or lost. God gives us time in sequence, one instant after another and never simultaneously. We only experience the present moment. God never reverses the orderly progression of time. God does not ask for more than we can handle in one moment.

I can almost hear you expressing regret. "What can I do? If what you say is true, how can I account for each moment God has already given me? I am now twenty-four years old and I haven't paid any attention to how I used my time. Even if I wanted to, I could not repair any past moment. The past remains as far beyond my reach as the future. Will tomorrow be any different? My own spiritual slowness traps me. For the love of Jesus, please help me."

You used the correct expression when you said "for the love of Jesus." The love of Jesus is the source of the help you need. Love's power brings everything together. Love Jesus, and everything of his becomes yours. As God made time, so God judges our use of time. Tie yourself to him with love and faith, knitting your relationship together. This way you may become a part of the larger fellowship of those fastened to God by love. You will have friends among the saints and angels who do not waste any time.

Pay attention and you will discover strength here. Try to understand what I am saying. But I offer one caution. You will not arrive at this relationship passively. God demands your personal involvement and dedication. Apply yourself diligently to both prayer and community responsibilities.

Notice, then, how contemplation affects your own soul. Genuine contemplation comes as a spontaneous, unexpected moment, a sudden springing toward God that shoots like a spark swirling up from a burning coal. A remarkable number of such moments may occur in an hour when the person in contemplation prepares properly and becomes familiar with this work. Any one of these sparkling moments may take on a unique quality resulting in a total detachment from the things of this world. On the other hand, earthly responsibilities and intrusions may tear you away from prayer. The thoughts of frail humans distract attention. Accept this as a natural experience. Your spiritual life receives no harm because of it. With practice, you may return immediately to profound prayer as another spark springs from the fire.

I have briefly summarized this experience of contemplation. Clearly, I report something quite different from fantasy, imagination, or subtle reasoning. Daydreaming is not the result of humble, devout love. A proud, speculative, and hyper-imaginative mind results in religious pretense. Control and subdue such elaborate notions.

Whoever reads or hears the directions given in this book may conclude that I am describing mental effort. But taxing your brain in an attempt to figure ways to achieve this produces nothing. Intellectual curiosity will lead you to dangerous self-deception. Unless God mercifully pulls you away from such a course, you may quickly fall into harmful frenzies and other spiritual sins that are works of the devil. May God lead you to an experienced, competent spiritual director who can guide you. For the love of God, be careful when you attempt contemplative prayer. Leave your senses and your imagination at rest, because there is no function for them here.

When I refer to this exercise as "darkness" or a "cloud," do not compare it with the darkness in your house when the candle burns out, or with a cloud in the sky that is composed of water vapor. Anyone can imaginatively conceive of that kind of darkness and cloud, even in broad daylight. I am not talking about such things.

Darkness results from a lack of knowledge, something unknown to you. What obscures God from you is not a cloud in the sky, but the *cloud of unknowing*.

CHAPTER 5

The cloud of forgetting

If you want to enter, live, and work in this *cloud of unknowing*, you will need a *cloud of forgetting* between you and the things of this earth. Consider the problem carefully and you will understand that you are farthest from God when you do not ignore for a moment the creatures and circumstances of the physical world. Attempt to blank out everything but God.

Even valuable thoughts of some special creatures are of little use for this exercise. Memory is a kind of spiritual light that the eye of the soul focuses upon, similar to the way an archer fixes his gaze upon a target. I tell you, whatever you think about looms above you while you are thinking about it, and it stands between you and God. To the extent that anything other than God is in your mind, you are that much farther from God.

I will also say, with reverence and respect, that regarding this exercise, even thinking about the kindness and worthiness of God, of any other spiritual being, or of the joys of heaven contributes nothing. These are uplifting and worthy subjects, but you are far better off contemplating God's pure and simple being, separated from all his divine attributes.

CHAPTER 6

A brief dialogue

You ask me, "How can I think about God in this elemental way?"

I reply, "I don't know. Your question has wrapped me in the same darkness, that *cloud of unknowing*, I wish you were in. It is possible for us to have extensive knowledge of many subjects, even theology. We have no difficulty thinking about such things. But we are incapable of thinking of God himself with our inadequate minds. Let us abandon everything within the scope of our thoughts and determine to love what is beyond comprehension. We touch and hold God by love alone.

"Therefore, while thinking about God's kindness and holiness may sometimes be worthwhile, these thoughts must be subdued (covered with a *cloud of forgetting*) in your time of contemplation. Have the courage to step above such ideas with loving devotion. Pierce that thick *cloud of unknowing* with a sharp dart of longing love. Do not turn away no matter what happens."

CHAPTER 7
Intellectual curiosity

Suppose a thought nags your mind, placing itself between you and that darkness, asking you, "What do you want? Who do you seek?" Give this answer: "I want God. I am looking for God, only God."

And if the thought persists, asking you, "Who is the God you seek?" answer saying, "The God who made me, redeemed me, and led me to this moment." Speak to your mind, "Thoughts, you cannot contain God. You have limited skill and you offer no assistance. Be silent!" Ignore the activity of your mind by devoutly turning to Jesus, even if your thoughts appear to be holy thoughts.

Quite likely, you will imagine your ideas are helpful. Many excellent and wonderful aspects of Christ's kindness, graciousness, and mercy spring up in your mind. They appear positive and worthy of your consideration, but as the mental chatter continues, it drags you down lower and lower, diverting your attention. Remember the Passion of Christ. This will lead you to recall your sinful past life. Memories of earlier times and places will flood into your awareness, scattering you in many directions; your concentration will be lost. This happened because you deliberately listened, responded, accepted, and allowed the thought to continue.

Still, these may be good and holy thoughts, essential elements as you begin meditation. You need to ponder frequently your own wretchedness, the Passion of Christ, and the kindness, extraordinary goodness, and dignity of God. Unless you do this, frustration will disturb your contemplation. With experience, you will learn to let distracting thoughts rest under a *cloud of forgetting* and attempt to penetrate the *cloud of unknowing* separating you from God.

Therefore, when God leads you to engage in the exercise described here, gently lift up your heart to God with love. Rest your thoughts only on the God who created you, redeemed you, and led you to this moment. Avoid any other thoughts of God. Direct a naked desire toward God.

You may wish to reach out to God with one simple word that expresses your desire. A single syllable is better than a word with two or more. "God" and "love" provide excellent examples of such words. Once you have selected the word you prefer, permanently bind this word to your heart. This word becomes your shield and spear in combat and in peace. Use this word to beat upon the cloudy darkness above you and to force every stray thought down under a *cloud of forgetting*. If a nagging thought pesters you, strike it with this monosyllabic word. If your mind begins to analyze the intellectual ramifications of your chosen word, remember that the value of this word is its simplicity. Do not allow the word to become fragmented. If you keep it intact, I can assure you distractions will soon diminish.

CHAPTER 8

Regarding uncertainties

Now you ask, "How do I evaluate these ideas that intrude upon my meditation? Are they good or evil? I doubt that they are evil, because they serve ordinary devotion so well. These thoughts bring pleasure. I have wept bitterly in sympathy with Christ and sometimes because of my awareness of my own wretched condition; this is a sacred and worthwhile experience. I can't consider such self-knowledge evil. If these thoughts do so much good for me, then why do you instruct me to press them down until they are out of sight beneath a *cloud of forgetting*?"

You ask an excellent question that I will try to answer. You want me to identify and label the thoughts that engage your mind in this exercise. You are thinking clearly, and each idea seems inherently good because you are reflecting the image of God.

Your use of each thought is critically important. The idea becomes good or evil in the application. Good results when God's grace enlightens you, enabling you to perceive your spiritual hunger and the wonderful kindness of God's activity. Your devotion increases. But if the thought makes you proud and arrogant, evil results follow. When you attempt subtle, theological speculation and vainly seek recognition as a scholar, rather than seeking devout humility, then you have lost thinking's most valuable aspect. Anyone who wants to appear clever and knowledgeable in any academic discipline, religious or secular, merely seeks flattery.

You also ask about the value of a *cloud of forgetting*. If such good thoughts assist a spiritual experience, why abandon them? The explanation lies in the difference between active and contemplative Christian living. Both activity and contemplation are essential and interrelated. You cannot fully experience one without the other, even though they have differences in character. The effectively active person is also contemplative. A contemplative person engages in Christian activity. The distinction between the two is that the active life begins and ends in this world, while the contemplative life begins here and continues eternally. Jesus told Martha, who was busy in the kitchen, that her sister, Mary, had chosen what is better, and she would never lose it. Active Martha is troubled and anxious about many things, but contemplative Mary sits in peace, intent only upon him.

At an elemental level, the active life engages in good and honest works of love and mercy. When the active life reaches higher expression, it shares good, spiritual meditation with the lower part of the contemplative life. But the higher part of the contemplative life, to the limited degree it may be experienced here, consists entirely in this darkness and this *cloud of unknowing*. It is an impulse of love, a dark gazing into the pure being of God.

In the beginning of the active life, we look beyond ourselves and work for others. As we progress in Christian activity, we begin to ponder the things of the spirit, but we remain within ourselves. But in the higher degree of the contemplative life, we rise above ourselves. We arrive by grace where we cannot go by nature. We unite with God in spirit, sharing his love, and we are in harmony with God's will.

As we cannot come to the higher part of the active life without pausing our business in the lower part, so we cannot come to the higher degree of the contemplative life without moving away from the elementary stages. Even holy works interfere with meditation. Similarly, you will find it inappropriate and cumbersome to think profound holy thoughts while working in this darkness of the *cloud of unknowing*.

For this reason, I advise you to suppress such pleasant thoughts, covering them with a thick *cloud of forgetting*, regardless of the apparent high quality of your ideas. In this life, love is the only way to reach God. Knowledge does not assist us. As long as the soul lives in this mortal body, the clarity of our understanding in the contemplation of spiritual things, particularly of God, mingles with imagination, tainting the experience and leading us into great error.

CHAPTER 9

Contemplative prayer

Resist intense mental activity when seeking this dark contemplation. Intellectual activity will hinder you. When you want to be alone with God, the conceptualizations of your mind will sneak into play. Rather than this darkness, our intellectual ability prefers a clear picture of something less than God. Such mental images, as pleasant as they may be, stand between you and God. Resist them.

For the health of your soul, pleasing God, and helping others, engage in a blind impulse of love toward God alone, a secret love beating on this *cloud of unknowing*. Seeking God this way is superior to seeing all the angels and saints in heaven, or hearing the laughter and music of those in bliss.

If you experience divine contemplation once on this level, you will agree I am not exaggerating. There is no way you will ever have a clear vision of God in this life, but you can have the gracious feeling I describe, if God grants it. Therefore, lift up your love to that cloud. More accurately, let God draw your love up to that cloud. Let God's grace help you to forget everything other than God. If all you are seeking is God, you will not be content with anything else.

CHAPTER 10

Discernment

When you are contemplating, thoughts about others fall into another category. Distractions may arrive unconsciously, beyond your control. Such thoughts may result in pleasure or grief. Human nature is frail. Quickly reject these thoughts; otherwise you will begin to experience positive or negative emotional responses and lose your stability. A memory of some pleasant past experience may trigger delight. A painful thought may make you angry.

If you have forsaken the world and committed yourself to a devout life, a temporary lapse does no harm. Root your intentions in God. Lingering with other thoughts allows them to intrude upon your spiritual experience. Consenting to them exposes you to the risk of falling into one of the seven deadly sins. For instance, if you willingly think of someone who has troubled you and you begin to conceive of ways to get even, *wrath* may result. *Envy* follows when you rashly develop a loathing contempt for another person. Or maybe you become weary of a good occupation and want to avoid it. *Sloth* then traps you. If you enjoy thinking about yourself, your achievements and attractiveness, *pride* waits at your elbow. Dwelling on material possessions you wish were yours becomes *covetousness*. If you cannot get your mind off delightful food and drink, you experience *gluttony*. When your thoughts concern the pleasures of love and flattery, or the seduction of another person, you *lust*.

CHAPTER 11
Evaluating thoughts

The purpose of my comments is not to place a burden of guilt on you. I want you to evaluate carefully each thought that stirs in your mind when you contemplate God. If an idea leads to sin, put a stop to it immediately. If you become careless about your early thoughts, you will have greater difficulty later. Everyone sins, but watch out for increasing sinfulness. True disciples can always avoid carelessness. Neglecting simple things prepares you for worse sins.

CHAPTER 12

Results of contemplation

To have a solid footing and to avoid stumbling, consistently puncture the *cloud of unknowing* that is between you and God with a sharp dart of longing love. Avoid thinking of anything less than God, and do not quit your time of contemplation regardless of what may happen. Loving contemplation destroys our tendency to sin more effectively than any other practice. Contemplation is superior to your fasts and vigils, regardless of how early in the morning you get up, the hardness of your bed, or the roughness of your hair shirt. Even if it were lawful for you to blind yourself, cut your tongue from your mouth, plug up your ears and nose, cut off your limbs and become a eunuch, none of these physical tortures would be of any value to you. The impulse to sin would still be in you.

Moreover, regardless of how much you fret about your sins in your straying thoughts or think of the joys of heaven, what do you gain? All of the value you gain from such practices fades when compared with the impulse of love. This, without anything else, is what Jesus described as Mary's "best part." When detached from loving desire, religious practices have little or no spiritual results.

Not only does contemplation destroy, as much as possible, our propensity to sin, it also attracts virtue. You will attract and absorb pure virtue when you truly seek God. Without love, any virtue you may already have will be tainted and imperfect.

Genuine goodness, after all, involves a unified, controlled love for God alone. All virtue is a gift of God, and two virtues, humility and love, include all the others. When we have these two, we have them all.

CHAPTER 13

Perfect and imperfect humility

Perfect humility comes from God. Humility from any other source means imperfection. To understand this, try to comprehend the true nature of humility.

Humility results from an honest personal appraisal. Nothing humbles us more than seeing ourselves clearly. Self-knowledge involves two steps. The first is an admission of our sinful nature. Regardless of our attempts to live a holy life, we cannot escape an awareness of our weak and fallen condition. The other source of our humility results from the recognition of the transcendent love and worthiness of God. Before God, nature trembles, the most educated become fools, and the saints and angels turn away from the brightness. God's presence inspires awe, and if God did not sustain us during the experience of it, unthinkable things might happen.

Perfect humility results from firsthand experience of God's goodness, and it lasts forever. Imperfect humility that springs from self-evaluation soon passes away, not only when we die, but also during those inspired moments when God allows an individual to rise above self-awareness. Whether this happens frequently or infrequently, it lingers for only a brief moment. During that instant, perfect humility is ours.

I do not intend to denigrate the first motive with the label "imperfect." Do not misinterpret what I am saying. You discover something of importance when you perceive your personal shortcomings.

CHAPTER 14

Begin with imperfect humility

I do not intend to denigrate the importance of honest self-knowledge when I speak of "imperfect" humility. Self-knowledge effectively helps me toward perfect humility, more so than having all the saints and angels in heaven, and having all living Christians pray constantly for me to obtain perfect humility. In fact, perfect humility is impossible without what I call "imperfect" humility.

Therefore, seek true knowledge of yourself. Eventually, you will arrive at a true knowledge and experience of God to the degree allowed to a humble soul still living in a mortal body.

Do not take my two divisions of humility (imperfect and perfect) as a directive to ignore the one and seek the other. I am explaining the extraordinary value of contemplative prayer, and how secret love, lifted in purity of spirit to the dark *cloud of unknowing* that exists between you and God, truly contains perfect humility without any special apprehension of anything less than God. If you know how to identify perfect humility, it becomes a signpost in your awareness. Lack of knowledge often results in pride.

If you do not understand perfect humility, your incomplete knowledge allows you to imagine you have already discovered it. Deceiving yourself, you might think you possess extreme humility while remaining immersed in foul, stinking pride. Strive for perfect humility. When you have it, you will not commit sin. Once you have experienced a moment of perfect humility, you will remain less susceptible to temptation.

CHAPTER 15

Understanding humility

Some mistakenly teach that remembering our despicable sins is the best path to perfect humility. Perfect humility exists, and God may allow you the experience, but introspection is not the best way to receive it.

True, for habitual sinners, a memory of past sins is spiritually useful. We are encrusted by a "rust" of sin. Our conscience and our spiritual director need to scour it away. On the other hand, some people naturally behave well and do not deliberately sin. Their sin is the result of weakness and lack of understanding. And yet, even these almost innocent ones who attempt a life of contemplative prayer have good reason for humility. Motivation toward humility comes from something far above imperfect self-knowledge. The goodness and love of God transcend imperfect motivation. Our Lord Jesus Christ tells us in the Gospel to be perfect by God's grace even as he is perfect by nature.

CHAPTER 16

Contemplative humility

There is no audacity in lovingly reaching out to God in the darkness of that *cloud of unknowing* between you and God. If you repent and experience a call to a life of contemplation, God welcomes you. Jesus told the sinful woman who washed his feet with her tears and dried them with her hair, "Your sins are forgiven." Divine forgiveness was not the result of her great sorrow, or her conviction of sin, or her perception of her own wretchedness. The Scripture tells us that Jesus said it because "she loved much." Study this biblical incident and see what a hidden impulse of love can elicit from our Lord.

Now there is no doubt that she regretted her sins and felt humility. Her deep sorrow was bundled together and carried perpetually in the recesses of her heart. She could never forget her sins. And yet, Scripture affirms that she had a greater sorrow provoked by her lack of love. She languished with sorrowing desire, sighing deeply, though her love was already strong. This should not surprise us, because the more we love, the more we want to love.

What did she do? Did she move down from the heights of her great desire and wallow in the memory of her failures? Did she search under every stone in the foul-smelling bog and dunghill of her life history? Did she dredge up her sins, one by one, sorrowing and weeping over each? No. Absolutely not. Why? Because God helped her to understand, by the grace in her soul, that this would not help anything.

She did the very opposite. She hung up her love and her longing desire in this *cloud of unknowing* and attempted to learn to love something she might never clearly perceive in this life, neither by intellectual insight nor by a true feeling of sweet, affectionate love. As a result, she paid little attention to whether or not she had been a sinner. The Lord's divinity moved her so much that she paid little attention to his physical appearance, as he stood right in front of her, speaking and teaching. The biblical narrative leads to the deduction that she remained insensible of anything other than his godliness.

CHAPTER 17

A critical world

St. Luke's Gospel reports a visit our Lord made to the home of Martha and Mary. While Martha busily prepared food for him, her sister sat at his feet. Listening to Jesus consumed all of Mary's attention, and she had no time for busy activity. Martha's active work was good and holy, representing the first stage of the active life. Mary experienced the second stage of the active life and the first of the contemplative life. Mary concentrated on the supreme and sovereign wisdom of God cloaked by his humanity. Nothing disturbed her. She sat perfectly still at the feet of Jesus with a secret love joyfully beating upon the high *cloud of unknowing* that hovered before God.

I repeat, the only way to approach God is through this *cloud of unknowing*. Mary directed the secret yearning of her heart to this cloud. She experienced the best and holiest part of contemplation. She would not be distracted even when Martha complained to Jesus about her inactivity. Mary sat with Jesus silently, not attempting to answer Martha. She did not even frown in response to her sister's complaint. She was busy with another kind of work.

Friend, the New Testament relates this story for our benefit. Mary and Martha represent Christian contemplation and Christian activity. Mary exemplifies all contemplative personalities in every generation.

CHAPTER 18

Ignorance

In the same way that Martha complained about her sister, Mary, active persons will continue to express concern about the behavior of contemplatives. Whenever anyone turns aside from the business of the world in order to give more time to prayer and meditation, others who do not share this interest will grumble. Family and friends will speak out sharply against what they interpret as "idleness." Because they do not observe any outward activity, they assume nothing is happening. They will mention many instances (some of them true) of how other people they know about have followed the contemplative path into ruin, but will fail to mention any positive examples.

Yes, some have negative experiences while attempting a contemplative life. Dangerous risks lurk in the shadows. The devil lures away some as they seek God, because they will not listen to a reliable spiritual director. These people then become heretics and hypocrites. They fall into frenzies and other kinds of mischief, discrediting the Holy Church.

I will not digress on this issue now because I want to continue with our central topic. If it seems necessary, I may return to this subject later, giving you the reasons why such things happen.

CHAPTER 19
Complaining

Perhaps you think I am denigrating Martha, that special saint. I do not mean to dishonor her any more than I wish to speak disparagingly of those active people who do not fully comprehend and appreciate contemplatives. God forbid that you construe anything written in this book as casting scorn on any of God's servants. Martha had every right to complain that Mary was not helping her prepare lunch. When she spoke, Martha was not aware of the spiritual depth of her sister's moment with Jesus Christ. Her complaint resulted from ignorance. We may excuse her.

In the same way, we should excuse those who complain about our contemplative life, even if they speak rudely. Make allowances for their ignorance. As Martha could not perceive what occupied Mary, neither can those in the world comprehend what young disciples of God attempt when they turn away from the business of the world. If they did, they would not criticize.

I have acted and spoken inappropriately on many occasions because of ignorance. If I want God to excuse my thoughtlessness, let me be charitable and compassionate regarding the uninformed comments of others. Otherwise, I am not doing to others as I would have them do to me.

CHAPTER 20

God responds

Those attempting the contemplative life should not only excuse their critics, but also be so deeply immersed in prayer that they pay no attention to what others may say or do. Our example, Mary, conducted herself this way. Jesus will certainly do for us what he did for her.

What did he do? Notice that Martha addressed her complaint to our blessed Lord rather than to her sister. She asked him to encourage Mary to help her in the kitchen. Jesus, understanding Mary's deep immersion in contemplation, answered on her behalf. Rather than distract Mary, he spoke to Martha with gentle courtesy, defending the one fervently occupied with spiritual contemplation of God. "Martha, Martha." Speaking her name twice emphasizes the importance of response. He assured Martha that her busy work had value and importance, but that her sister engaged in a better enterprise. She was doing the one essential thing, the work of love and praising God alone. Activity and prayer mingle imperfectly, but Mary had discovered the perfect movement of love toward God. Similar in nature to heavenly bliss, divine contemplation already participates in eternity.

CHAPTER 21

The text

What does Christ mean when he says, "Mary has chosen the best part?" To designate something as "the best" implies that there is a good, a better, and a best. What then are our three options? There are not three types of lives because the church recognizes only two: active and contemplative. We may understand the story of these two sisters as an allegory describing each. No third possibility exists. We may not refer to either as "the best."

Though there are only two types of Christian living, each has three parts in varying degrees of quality. You may refer to my earlier explanation of these under the eighth heading. In the third degree of the contemplative life one experiences a dark *cloud of unknowing* where love centers privately and exclusively on God. This third stage is "the best" of all, the part Mary selected. Our Lord did not say that Mary had chosen the best manner of life, but rather that she selected the best part of two respected lives.

This best part is eternal because heaven has no need for acts of mercy. No one will be hungry or thirsty, no one will be sick or die of coldness, no one will be homeless or in jail. If God calls you to choose as Mary did, then respond wholeheartedly. Beginning here, contemplation endures forever.

The voice of Christ continues speaking to active Christians today. "Martha, Martha." We may express it this way: "Actives, actives, work hard at your merciful business now, but do not interfere with the work of contemplatives. You simply do not understand what they are doing. Leave them alone. Grant them the stillness and quiet of Mary's third and best part."

CHAPTER 22
Love and contemplation

Our Lord and Mary shared a sweet love. She greatly loved him, but he loved her even more. The account of Mary and Martha is far more than a romantic fable. Do not overlook the truth expressed in the Gospel: Mary loved Jesus so much that nothing less than his divinity could interest her. When she tearfully went to his sepulcher on Easter morning, not even angels could comfort her. They spoke to her tenderly, "Do not weep, Mary. The one you seek is risen, and you will see him again in all his beauty among his disciples in Galilee, as he promised." Even the angel's assurance was not enough to satisfy her. When we seek the king of angels, we do not settle for angels.

If you study the Scripture, you will discover other wonderful, instructive examples of this perfect love. Each narrative underscores and explains the message of this book. Study, understand, and apply them.

CHAPTER 23

God's spiritual provision

If we honestly attempt to emulate Mary's love and manner of living, God will answer those who do not understand what we are doing the way he answered for her. We will always have critics who will speak against us, as Martha spoke against Mary. Like Mary, we do not need to pay them any attention. Their comments need not interrupt our hidden spiritual activity. Our Lord will answer them in spirit, and they will soon be ashamed of what they said.

In the same way, God will inspire others to provide us with all that we need to sustain life. They will provide us with food, clothing, and everything else we require. I say this in order to refute the error some make in holding that we behave improperly when we devote ourselves to the service of God through a life of contemplation without already having a stockpile of earthly necessities. They quote the proverb, "God sends the cow, but not by the horn." They make a mistake when they say this about God. If you sincerely turn from the world to God, trust that God will give you either everything you need, or the patience to endure without it. What difference does it make which of the two you have? It does not matter. If you doubt this, either the devil is in your heart, robbing you of faith, or else your conversion to God is not complete.

Determine to become an authentic contemplative like Mary. Choose to be humbled by the magnificence of God, which is perfect, rather than by your own wretchedness, which is imperfect. Make God's worthiness the goal of your attention. Do not be distracted by your own miserable sinfulness. The perfectly humble will never lack material or spiritual essentials, because they have God, and God is everything. They need nothing else.

CHAPTER 24

Contemplative love

Humility is subtly and perfectly discovered in this blind little impulse of love that beats upon the dark *cloud of unknowing*, with everything else put completely out of mind. The same is true of all the other virtues, including the love of God alone, and loving others for God's sake as you love yourself. The essence of contemplation is a simple and direct reaching out to God. People who pray at this depth do not seek relief from pain nor do they seek increased rewards, but only the fulfillment of God's will. Nothing else shares this simple moment.

Thoughts of friend or foe do not distract the one absorbed in contemplation. Everyone is a friend, none a foe. Those who cause pain or grief become special friends.

CHAPTER 25

Details

Perfect contemplation does not allow space for special regard to anyone alive, whether friend or foe, family or stranger. One forgets anything other than God. Once this moment passes, prayer for others will be inclusive, caring equally for everyone. When I speak of the passing of the moment, I do not imply that we come down completely, but rather that we descend from the height of contemplation in order to perform activity required by love.

CHAPTER 26

When difficult prayer becomes possible

Devote yourself now to a time of contemplation. Beat upon this high *cloud of unknowing*. Rest will come later. This will be hard work, unless you receive a special grace. Let it become habitual from continual practice.

Why is contemplation of God a difficult, costly business? Certainly, no awakening of fervent love brings spiritual pain, because this is God's work and not our own. God is eager to activate a prepared soul.

What, then, necessitates the toil? We labor to eliminate the numerous distractions that pester us, placing them under a *cloud of forgetting*. While we will need God's help with this, we expend much energy. If you diligently practice your own assignment, I promise you, God will not fail you.

Get on with it now! Let me see how you are doing. Can't you see, God is waiting for you, encouraging you? Work hard for a while and you will soon find rest for your soul. Even though devotional beginners find the effort difficult, contemplative prayer will eventually become familiar and welcomed. The effort will become easy because God will sometimes work for you.

God may decide to send a ray of spiritual light to illumine the *cloud of unknowing* that stands between you. Within the ray he will reveal some of his unspeakable secrets. You will feel the fire of devotion in your affectionate soul more than I am willing or able to describe at this moment. I do not dare express with my babbling tongue the work that uniquely belongs to God. Instead of taking that risk, I simply encourage you to do your part.

CHAPTER 27
Who should attempt contemplation?

Primarily, I need to express clearly who should try contemplative prayer. Some personalities will find contemplation more suitable than others. It is a personal choice. Appropriate candidates are individuals with a sincere desire to forsake the world. It does not matter that such a seeker may have been a habitual sinner earlier in life. Everyone who has the desire should devote attention to this exercise.

CHAPTER 28
Begin by seeking forgiveness

The first step toward divine contemplation involves cleansing your conscience from sins you know you have committed, following the regular practices of the Holy Church.

This will destroy the root and ground of sin in the soul. If you are ready to start, first purify your conscience. When you have done all you can, according to church practices, you may boldly, but humbly, begin. Tarry no longer.

As long as you live in this mortal flesh, you will always see and feel this thick *cloud of unknowing* between yourself and God. Many things and people will consistently intrude upon your meditation. This is God's judgment on our sinful nature, because when we were in a position above all other creatures in the Garden of Eden, Adam willfully disobeyed his Creator. Now the creatures that should be beneath us are proudly harassing us

CHAPTER 29
Endurance

Everyone finds contemplation difficult, regardless of personal experience. We reasonably expect that people who come from a sinful life will struggle the most in an attempt to begin contemplation, but it often happens that some who have been wicked and habitual sinners arrive more quickly at this moment of perfection than those who have not. This is a miracle of mercy from our Lord, who gives his grace in this special way, astonishing worldly observers.

Honestly, I anticipate Judgment Day with delight because the goodness of God will become sparkling clear in all God's gifts. Then, some whom the world despises and considers to be of little account, perhaps even some wicked sinners, will take their rightful place with God among his saints. Some who now appear holy and receive honor for their angelic behavior will sadly take their place among those rejected when God separates the sheep from the goats.

Judging others, pronouncing them good or bad, is God's business. We may evaluate behavior, but not the person.

CHAPTER 30

Critics

Is there anyone qualified to pass judgment on the behavior of others?

Certainly, those who have controlled their own souls, either by the external authority of the church, or by the internal impulse of the Holy Spirit, may lovingly judge. We must be careful not to condemn others unless that is our calling to a special religious position. Likely, we will make mistakes in judgment. Be cautious. Judge yourself before God as much as you want, but leave others to the judgment of God.

CHAPTER 31
Beginners and temptation

After you have done everything possible to amend your life according to the rules of the Holy Church, earnestly attempt contemplation. If memory of your past sins continues to bar your approach to the divine, or new thoughts prompt you to sin, bravely crush them. Step over every obstacle in your way with a fervent impulse of love, squashing them beneath your feet. Cover these temptations with a thick *cloud of forgetting*, as though they never occurred.

Suppress negative thoughts as often as they arise. The more they trouble you, the more you will be motivated to look for special means of control. You will discover tricks and techniques that help you put them away. The inspiration of God is the best teacher of these tactics.

CHAPTER 32

Spiritual devices

My own experience provides two techniques that can help you cope with distractions. I suggest you experiment with them. Improve them if you can.

Exert firm resolve to act as though you did not notice spurious ideas. Try to ignore the fact that hindering thoughts are barging into your time of prayer and coming between you and God. Look far beyond spurious thoughts, seeking God instead. If you persist resolutely, you will soon find it easier to focus your attention. At its root, this first technique is nothing other than a longing for God. You want to experience God as intimately as possible in this earthly life. Such desire is an expression of love, and love always deserves fulfillment.

The opposite approach also works. If you feel helpless and are not able to control your thoughts, cringe like a coward in battle. Admit the impossibility of ignoring intrusive thoughts and the futility of struggling against them anymore. In the act of placing yourself in the hands of your enemies, you will also give yourself up to God. Relax as though you are hopelessly defeated. This method is certainly worth trying. When you experiment with it, you will feel as though you are melting in water. If you understand the subtlety of this device, it is nothing other than acceptance of yourself as you truly are. Humility of this kind will attract God to your defense in the same way a father rescues a child from the mouths of wild boars and enraged, biting bears. God will tenderly blot your spiritual tears.

CHAPTER 33
Perfect rest

I will not attempt to teach you any other contemplative methods now. If God's grace assists you while experimenting with the two I have mentioned, you will become able to teach me better than I can teach you. I still have a long way to go and I pray that you will help me. Work for yourself and for me.

Get started now and stick with it for a while. If you are not able to succeed immediately, endure your distress with humility. God is purging you. When the pain subsides, and your desire is granted, and contemplation becomes habitual, your sin will no longer cause you grief. You remain a sinner, but that general fact will not trouble you as much as you have grieved over your personal sins.

The hard work will never cease, because fresh temptations will continue to spring from original sin. You will always need to cultivate your spiritual life. There is no absolute security or any complete rest in this world. Keep at it! Don't give up!

CHAPTER 34

God's gift

You desire guidance regarding how to engage in this work of loving contemplation. I pray that God himself will teach you. It pleases God to work graciously in your soul. You do not earn a gift. God decides who will receive this mercy. God works as he wishes, where he chooses, and when it pleases him.

God does not begin this work in the soul that does not have the capacity for contemplation. Innocence and guilt have nothing to do with God's gift of grace. God gives freely to one and withholds from another in proportion to spiritual capacity. Notice that I say "withholds," rather than "withdraws." Be careful to avoid serious error here. The nearer we approach the truth, the more we need to guard against mistaken ideas. If what I am saying is correct, but does not make any sense to you, then let my instruction rest until God opens your understanding. Otherwise, you may trip into spiritual snags.

Guard yourself against personal pride. Pride blasphemes God's gifts and produces arrogant sinners. Humility will help you understand my teaching. Working at contemplation characteristically gives the soul the capacity to possess and experience higher prayer. The soul's capacity depends upon an awareness of the presence of God. The capacity and the exercise itself are inseparable. Apart from the grace of God, you would be insensitive to the reality of contemplative prayer and would have no inclination toward it. Your experience depends upon your eagerness. You will never want to engage in divine contemplation until the inexpressible and unknowable prompts you.

Do not be distracted by pondering the spiritual ramifications of contemplation. Simply continue constant prayerful contemplation. Let the process work in you, leading where it will. Be passive as contemplation becomes active, an observer rather than a participant. You can do nothing to help, and your interference will spoil everything. Think of yourself as wood in a carpenter's hands, or as a house in which someone else lives. Control your curiosity. Be satisfied with knowing that you are being motivated to love by something you may not comprehend. God directs your activity of reaching out to God.

If your experience confirms what I am saying, you may be confident that God is personally involved with you. No other force is involved. Do not fear the devil because he will never approach this closely and motivate to this degree, regardless of his cleverness. Neither can an angel directly affect your soul. Only God can accomplish what is happening to you.

Experience will demonstrate that in contemplation we have no need of special techniques. Orderly procedures are worthless. The best methods depend upon God's activity, but God's activity depends on nothing.

CHAPTER 35

Reading, reflection, and prayer

Nevertheless, you can do three things to prepare yourself as an apprentice contemplative. You can read a passage of Scripture, reflect upon what you have read, and pray. Other books describe and explain this better than I can here. It is enough for me to remind you that these three—reading, reflection, and prayer—are mutually dependent. There cannot be any profitable reflection without preparation by reading or hearing, and true prayer springs only from previous reflection.

God's word, whether read or heard, functions as a mirror. The spiritual eye of the soul is the ability to reason. Conscience places the spiritual eye in a face. As your physical eyes cannot see dirt on your face without a mirror, neither can your spiritual eyes discover the truth without the reflection of Scripture. Unless you read or listen to God's word, you will never perceive your frailty.

When you see dirt in a physical or spiritual mirror, you go to the well to wash. If a particular sin blemishes you, the Holy Church provides the well, and confession in the manner approved by the church functions as water. If the stain is only a blind root with a tendency toward sinful behavior, then a merciful God becomes the well. Prayer in its fullest dimension serves as water.

You can see, therefore, that for both beginners and advanced contemplatives, reading or hearing the word of God comes first, deep reflection on the text follows, and serious prayer comes next.

CHAPTER 36

Meditation

Those who are habitually engaged in contemplation have a different experience. Their meditations arrive suddenly without additional preparation. Spontaneous awareness of this kind originates with God.

You are not obligated to engage in meditations on your own sinfulness or God's goodness, provided you feel yourself moved to contemplation by grace in conformity with your director's spiritual guidance. Repeating single words, such as "sin" or "God," stimulates contemplation. There is no need to analyze or interpret the word you select. Logical reasoning could not possibly increase your devotion. Let the word remain in a single lump, a part of yourself.

When you think of the significance of a word like "sin," consider it as a total condition rather than as particular behaviors. This larger perspective ought to be enough to make you behave like an insane person, but anyone observing you will see nothing unusual, whether you are sitting, walking, lying down, leaning on something, standing, or kneeling. You will appear sober and peacefully resting.

CHAPTER 37

Special prayers

Spontaneity characterizes the prayerful meditation of those who frequently contemplate God in private. Those who are deeply involved with contemplation have high regard for the church's prayers, and they use them regularly in the manner prescribed by earlier generations. Their personal prayers, however, are spontaneous, rising directly to God without external prompting. Words are rarely used. As I suggested in the previous section, a little word of only one syllable is enough, opening your spirit to the strongest work of the Holy Spirit.

Let me explain this with an illustration from common human experience. When a life-threatening situation frightens someone, that person will usually cry out involuntarily. In pain or terror, we do not use complete sentences, and probably not even an actual word of one or two syllables. Such a moment does not allow expressing one's needs in lengthy comment. We break out in a loud and shocking scream. Perhaps we will shout, "Fire!" or "Help!"

In the same way that little shouts and gasps catch the attention of bystanders, a little word, spoken or thought, conceived in the profundity of the spirit, bursts upon the attention of God. As an aid to meditation, a single word functions better than a long psalm mumbled inarticulately. Christ taught us in Matthew's Gospel that spoken prayers are best when they are not too long.

CHAPTER 38

Why short prayers pierce heaven

A little prayer of one syllable pierces heaven because we concentrate our entire spiritual energy into it. One little gasp contains the height, depth, width, and breadth of the spirit. With a single syllable, we begin to comprehend the lesson that St. Paul and all the saints glimpsed concerning the vastness of God's love, power, and knowledge.

We are not surprised, then, that when a soul conforms this closely by grace to the image and likeness of its Creator, God quickly notices. Even if the expression originates in a sinful soul, in an enemy of God, the terrible noise of this cry will receive divine response.

You run to help anyone who screams an alarming cry, regardless of whether that person is your friend or your enemy. Pity stirs your emotions, and you will get up, even on a cold winter night, to assist the one calling for help.

O Lord! If we can become so merciful by grace toward an enemy, what pity and mercy will you have in response to a spiritual cry of the soul, uttered in the height, depth, length, and breadth of the Spirit? God will act more certainly beyond any comparison with human behavior.

CHAPTER 39

The nature of prayer

Find a repeatable word compatible with the nature of prayer. If you understand prayer, you will be able to select a proper word more easily.

The essence of prayer is a devout intention directed to God to reduce evil and increase good. The word "sin" summarizes all evil. "God" is the epitome of good. These are marvelously compact words with profound content. If God ever leads me to shorter words with this much meaning, I will use them instead. You should do the same.

Do not waste time searching for the right word. If God inspires you to use one of the two I have mentioned, then do it. If you think of a better word, adopt it for your own use. If you would rather pray with no word at all, then ignore what I have said.

Though I highly recommend brief prayer, there is no limit on the frequency of prayer. Pray in the dimension of the Spirit, never stopping until you find what you are seeking. The person in great distress will continue calling for help until someone hears and responds. Pray until you penetrate the *cloud of unknowing*.

CHAPTER 40

Forgetting virtue and vice

When you fill your spirit with the spiritual significance of the word "sin," do not concentrate on particular sins (pride, anger, envy, covetousness, sloth, gluttony, or lust). A contemplative soul does not care which sin, or how great a sin may corrupt its experience. During the time of contemplation, all sins are equal because even the "smallest" sin gets in the way.

Think of sin as a lump. You do not need to identify or classify particular behaviors, because it is enough to acknowledge you are sinful. Repeat the same cry, "Sin, sin, sin! Out, out, out!" God is the best teacher of this spiritual cry. Its perfection rests in its purity of spirit. In the same way, the little word "God" can flood your spirit with spiritual meaning without giving attention to particular activities of God.

Moreover, have no regard for any virtue that God's grace might give you. Thinking about humility, charity, patience, abstinence, hope, faith, temperance, chastity, or voluntary poverty is counterproductive. Spiritual virtues simply do not matter to contemplatives. All virtues discovered and experienced are in God. Contemplatives know that if they have God they will have everything that is good. Rather than focusing on anything in particular, they concentrate on God alone. Let God's grace help you do the best you can with this. Think only of God. Seek nothing other than God.

Alternating between "sin" and "God" will help you understand an important spiritual lesson. If you have God, you would not have sin. If you were without sin, you could have God.

CHAPTER 41

Contemplation and indiscretion

You do not have any freedom to practice moderation during contemplation. You choose how you do everything else, such as eating, drinking, sleeping, dressing according to the weather, the length of your prayers, study, and conversation. In these things, you decide how much is too much or too little. But in contemplation, there are no limits. Engage in it tirelessly for the rest of your life.

I do not mean that you will always contemplate with uniform depth. Illness or other circumstances will demand your energy, pulling you down from spiritual heights. For the love of God, take care of yourself and try to avoid sickness. Never do anything that will endanger your health. To contemplate God as I am describing, both your body and your soul need to be in good shape. Do the best you can to preserve the health of both.

If unexpected sickness comes to you, be patient and humbly wait for God's mercy. You can do nothing else. Patience when you are ill pleases God more than the kind of devotion you might express when you are well.

CHAPTER 42

Indiscretion produces discretion

You want to know how you may practice discretion in all the activities of your life. I have a brief answer: Do the best you can with what you have. Contemplate in depth and you will know where to begin and end everything else you do. If you persevere in prayerful contemplation day and night, you will never use poor judgment in the physical world, unless you are a bungler who never gets anything right.

If I could be absorbed and faithful all of the time, then eating, drinking, sleeping, speaking, or any other outward activity would become less important. I would enjoy freedom from the demands of such things. Others may express another point of view, but my experience declares that indiscretion in contemplation results in worldly discretion.

Lift up your heart, then, with a blind impulse of love, pondering "sin" and "God." You are seeking God and desire to eliminate sin. What you lack now is God and what you surely have is sin. May the good God help you.

CHAPTER 43
Forgetting the self

Let nothing stir your mind or will other than God. Attempt to suppress all your thoughts and feelings regarding subjects less than God. Put distracting ideas under a *cloud of forgetting*. In contemplation, forget everything, including yourself and your accomplishments.

Be impatient with everything that stirs in your mind other than God. Anything else will hinder your approach to God. Reject every thought and memory of all things, particularly yourself. Your own experiences and desires will be the most difficult to eliminate. This personal knowledge and emotion will hinder your contemplative ability. Obliterate it.

CHAPTER 44

Suppressing the self

You can see that if you are able to destroy an awareness of your own being, all other hindrances to divine contemplation will also vanish. Only God's grace can accomplish the forgetting of the self. Prepare to receive this special gift. Otherwise, you cannot avoid this basic awareness of your being.

A strong, deep spiritual sorrow will prepare you. Be careful, while you have this sorrow, not to exert too much stress on your body and spirit. Relax and be comfortable as though you were falling asleep, exhausted with grief. This is true sorrow, perfect sorrow. You will be fortunate if you can discover such sorrow.

Everyone understands there is good reason to be sorrowful, but it comes most purely to the contemplative who earnestly grieves because of a consciousness not only of *what* he is but also *that* he is. If you have not felt the sorrow of your own existence, you have never experienced real sorrow. The sorrow that comes from knowing that you exist purifies you of sin and sin's consequences. It prepares you to receive the joy that is higher than the knowing and feeling of your existence.

Holy desire fills sorrow of this kind. If contemplation did not comfort the soul, the pain of being conscious of your existence would be unbearable. When we want a true knowledge and experience of God in purity of spirit, as much as this life permits, we realize satisfaction is beyond us, out of reach. The lump of our own being gets in the way. Recognizing this, we nearly go out of our minds with grief. We weep and wail, struggle and curse. We think we are bearing a burden so heavy that we do not even care what happens to us, if it pleases God.

In all this sorrow, we do not wish we were dead. That is the insanity of the devil and shows contempt for God. Instead, we are pleased to exist and we are sincerely grateful to God for the noble gift of being, even though we would like to lose awareness of our being.

Such sorrow and desire are natural elements of every soul's experience before a perfect, loving union with God.

CHAPTER 45

Spiritual illusions

During contemplation, deception comes easily to a young and inexperienced disciple. Unless you are aware of this at the beginning and are intelligent enough to seek spiritual direction, you will probably hurt yourself and become a victim of spiritual fantasy.

Here is how it happens. A young man or a woman who has started the study of devotion reads or hears about the sorrow and desire mentioned previously. They do not understand the spiritual intent of these words, but accept them at face value. They foolishly attempt to lift up the heart in their chests, straining their physical and emotional capacity. Instead of receiving the inspiration of God's grace, mere vanity and conceit excite them. Weariness soon sets in and the neophyte turns aside for rest and recreation.

If beginners escape this trap, they will probably burn with an unnatural religiosity that is directly opposed to spiritual exercise. Their imaginations create a false heat, as the devil plays on their pride, earthliness, and erroneous thought. They probably accept the experience as a genuine gift from the Holy Spirit. These religious illusions result in great trouble, hypocrisy, heresy, and error. False religious experience induces false knowledge in the same way that authentic devotion helps us to understand God's truth. There can be no denying that the devil has his contemplatives too.

False religious experience comes in many varieties. A catalog of religious illusions would be of little help for you now. I will not give additional descriptions of how educated theologians, men and women living a different life from yours, are deceived. My focus is exclusively on those who want to attempt divine contemplation at its purest level. What I have mentioned already will serve to guard you from stumbling into illusory traps.

CHAPTER 46
Spiritual enthusiasm

For the love of God, be careful not to injure yourself. Contemplation requires spiritual enthusiasm rather than brute force. Skill comes with humility. If you force elevated prayer, the results will be physical rather than spiritual. Take care. If you approach this work with the strength of an ox plowing a field, you will encounter stones that cause injury. Vulgar straining belongs to an effort of the flesh that is unfamiliar with divine grace, and the resulting devilish fantasies are harmful.

Instead of approaching contemplation compulsively, discover how to love God joyfully with a gentle and peaceful disposition of body and soul. Wait patiently for God. Be courteous. Don't tear into it like a hungry dog, no matter how eager you may be. Do everything you can to slow the process. Play a game, pretending you don't want God to perceive the depth of your desire to experience his presence. Am I speaking playfully and childishly? If you do as I say, you will discover the game well worth playing. A father plays with his child, kissing and embracing.

CHAPTER 47

Approaching God

For some time now, I have been thinking in this childish way. I have made these comments to close friends in God as well as to you on these pages.

One reason I encourage you to hide your desire from God is that I actually believe this act makes it even more visible to God. Additionally, I'm trying to bring you out of imperfect physical feeling and into the pure depth of spiritual feeling. I desire to help you tighten the spiritual knot of warm love that is between you and God, to lead you to spiritual unity with God.

You already know that God is a spirit, and whoever wants to be made one with him must live in spirit and in truth. You also know that God is omniscient and that nothing escapes his awareness, whether physical or spiritual. Since God is a spirit, God knows the hidden depths of the spirit even more clearly than experience soiled by sensory perception or human emotion. By nature, physical experiences are farther from God than spiritual experiences. When our spiritual desires mingle with physical qualities (as they do when we push ourselves too hard), we are disadvantaged.

Perhaps now you understand why I asked you to conceal your desire from God in this childish way. I am not telling you simply to hide it. I would be a fool if I thought you could do the impossible. I am instructing you to try every way you can to *attempt* to hide it. Put your spiritual desire down as far as you can into the depths of your spirit. Isolate your desire from influences that will contaminate it. The more refined your spiritual approach to God, the less human struggle and emotion. This pleases God and makes your desire more clearly visible. This is not to say that God can see one thing better than another. God perceives everything equally well. I am trying to say that a pure spiritual desire is more like God, who is spirit.

Another reason I want you to do everything you can to keep this desire hidden from God, is that you and I, and many others like us, tend to think of spiritual things in a physically sensible way. If I told you to reveal the spiritual stirrings of your heart to God, you may use a gesture, or spoken words, or some other bodily motion as though you were communicating with another person. This would degrade your devotional exercise. We speak one way with people, and another way with God.

CHAPTER 48

Physical aspects of prayer

My comments do not imply that you should quit contemplation if you suddenly feel a desire to pray with words or to express the devotion of your spirit openly. It is completely acceptable for phrases such as, "Good Jesus, lovely Jesus, sweet Jesus," and similar comments to be expressed. May God forbid that you misunderstand me.

God wants us to serve him properly with both body and spirit together. Both physical and spiritual rewards accrue. Sometimes God will stir the bodily senses of his devout servants. The sweet consolations of God do not arrive through the windows of our senses, but inwardly, rising and springing up out of abundance of spiritual joy and out of true spiritual devotion. The person experiencing them need not be suspicious of these good and natural pleasures.

The consolations worthy of our suspicion come suddenly from outside ourselves, with an uncertain origin. Be cautious regarding such external pleasures because they may be good or evil. If you follow my instruction by avoiding physical and psychological stress, the consolations that come to you will be neither evil nor harmful. Why? Because this comfort, this devout wakening of love in a pure spirit, comes from God alone, rather than an illusion or a mistaken notion.

I will not attempt now to tell you how to distinguish between good or evil comforts, sounds, and pleasures. You can find this topic discussed in another book a thousand times better than I could express it. For that matter, that other book contains everything I say here, but I will not let that discourage me from preparing this guide for you.

Constantly practice this simple, devout stirring of love that I have described. This love will inform you whether the sensual pleasure you experience is good or evil. Even if the pleasures confuse simple love in the beginning, you will not be able to pay much attention to them until you reach certainty about them, either inwardly by the Spirit of God, or outwardly by the guidance of your spiritual director.

CHAPTER 49

Essence of perfection

I urge you to follow eagerly this humble stirring of love
in your heart. Love functions as your guide in this world,
and it will bring you to grace in the next. Simple love is the
substance of all good living. Without love, you can neither
begin nor complete any good work. The essence of perfection is a good will directed toward God, and an experience
of pleasure in all that God does. All other pleasures, sensible
or spiritual, depend on the direction of your love.

I call the consolations of contemplation "accidentals,"
because it makes little difference whether they are present
or absent. In heaven's happiness, they unite with the devout
will without any lines of demarcation, even as our souls are
now united with our bodies. I am sure that anyone who
has matured in contemplative prayer has no joyful earthly
pleasure worth clinging to if God wants us to renounce it.

CHAPTER 50

Pure love

You can see the importance of giving all of your attention to this humble stirring of love in your will. Nothing else is worthy of your concentration. If other pleasures come, welcome them, but do not depend on them. If you enjoy spiritual pleasures too much, they will sap your strength. It could happen that you will be motivated to love God simply to enjoy such consolations. This twist has already occurred if you complain when the pleasures are absent. Perfect love does not grumble about withdrawn favors. Love is pleased to do without consolations if that is what God wants.

Some people have regular experiences of such spiritual comforts, but others experience them rarely. It depends upon God, who understands individual needs. Some of us are so weak that if we do not experience spiritual sweetness we cannot contend with the temptations and tribulations that come to us. Others are in poor health and unable to do penance for their own purification. The Lord does penance for them with sweet consolations and tears. For yet others, satisfaction comes through a reverent and humble stirring of love, accepting God's will. This group of contemplatives does not need emotional sustenance. Only God knows which of these conditions is the most holy. I do not.

CHAPTER 51

Misinterpretation

Humbly follow the sightless stirring of love in your heart. Again, I mean your spiritual "heart," the driving force of your will. Be careful not to interpret the things I say materially and literally. As I have said, the physical and sensual interpretations of those who chase after fancy result in many errors.

Remember how I asked you to hide your spiritual desire from God the best you can? If I had asked you to exhibit that desire openly, you might have interpreted me in a more material way. When I instruct you to hide it, you understand that what you keep as a secret you conceal deeply in your spirit.

Be careful in your interpretation of ordinary words that may carry spiritual meaning, such as "in" and "up." A misunderstanding of these words will draw you into illusion and erroneous thinking. I know this from my own experience, and from reports that have reached me.

A young disciple in God's school, newly converted from the world, begins to think that because he has given himself to penance and prayer for a little while, he may now begin the serious contemplation about which he has heard or read. When the text states that one should pull all understanding "within" and then rise "above" himself, the novice reader interprets this as meaning physical spatial relationships. With a natural curiosity about anything hidden, he immediately misinterprets the statement, concluding that God is inspiring him. If his spiritual director does not encourage him, he becomes unhappy. He complains to others who are in the same condition, that no one understands him. Without hesitation, and with arrogant intellectual pride, he abandons humble prayer and penance too soon, and begins to attempt true spiritual exercises within his soul.

Correctly understood, the spiritual practice this person begins is neither of the senses nor of the spirit, but rather an unnatural activity designed by the devil, deadly to body and soul, madness and not wisdom. The young disciple does not perceive this. He intends to think of nothing other than God.

CHAPTER 52

Beginners' mistakes

Beginners misapply what they read and hear about stopping outward exercises and working inwardly, because they are not sure what inward activity might be. They incorrectly attempt to turn their physical senses inward in an unnatural way, straining to look with physical eyes and hear with physical ears the sights and sounds of the Spirit. With damaging introspection, beginners stimulate all their senses, attempting to smell, taste, and touch inward things, a violently abusive practice. They damage their brains, giving the devil an opportunity to fabricate false lights, sounds, smells, tastes, and various sensations in their internal and external organs.

Beginners do not recognize these sensations as the devil's tricks. They think this is a tranquil awareness of God without any distraction by vain thoughts. The devil busily concocts the fantasy. He escapes detection by cleverly allowing his inexperienced victim to imagine he is contemplating God.

CHAPTER 53

Outward behavior

When compared with that of God's true disciples, the behavior of those misled into false contemplation appears strange. Instead of controlling themselves in a reserved manner, we may observe them with the wide, staring eyes of madness, as though they were seeing the devil. In fact, they had better be careful, because the devil is not far from them. Sometimes their eyes are set deeply in their heads, making them look like sheep with a brain disease, and near death. Sometimes they tilt their heads to one side as though they were trying to get a worm out of their ear. Some squeak instead of speaking normally, emulating shortness of breath. Hypocrites tend to behave as I describe. Some are so eager and quick to say what they think that they gurgle and splutter in their throats like heretics. They presumptuously and stubbornly cling to their erroneous ways, defending their behavior with clever explanations.

Anyone who watches them will see bizarre behavior that results from erroneous ideas. A few are clever enough to control themselves when others are watching, but if you could see them alone, their guard would be down and they would not be hiding their faults. When someone challenges or questions them, they react strongly. They are confident that everything they are doing is for the love of God. I expect they will go on loving God in this odd way until they go out of their minds, unless God mercifully instructs them to stop.

I do not know any single individual who is such a perfect servant of the devil that he exhibits all of the behavior I have mentioned, but we see many combinations. Hypocrites and heretics are inclined to behave that way. With God's help, I'll add some more odd behavior to the list.

Some misled people do strange things with their bodies. When they listen, they waggle their heads. Their mouths gape open as though their ears were inside. Others, when speaking, use their fingers to poke their own and their listeners' chests. They can neither sit, stand, nor lie still. They tap their feet, flex their fingers, and make rowing motions with their arms as though they were swimming instead of talking. Some laugh or smile with every other word, as though they were giggling adolescents. They remind me of off-balance amateur jugglers. This kind of happiness would be good and proper if it came with physical reserve and a joyful attitude.

Bizarre behavior is no sin in itself, and those who do things like this are not necessarily great sinners. It is simply not necessary, and can take control of an individual. It often becomes a sign of pride. Outlandish behavior can be a form of exhibitionism, especially if it comes from emotional instability.

Those engaged in spiritual exercises need to test themselves by the symptoms I have listed.

CHAPTER 54
Controlling the body

Those who are experienced in the practice of divine contemplation become both better looking and better companions. Contemplative prayer will transform the ugliest and most disagreeable person alive. Others seek and enjoy their company, sensing that they have discovered spiritual peace and, because of their companionship with God, have received strength in his grace.

Anyone who possesses true spirituality will know how to govern himself and how to deal with all of the attendant blessings. This is a gift worth receiving. He will be able to understand others, and will know how to relate with them in positive ways. God will work through him, attracting others to a life of prayer. His appearance and comments will be spiritually lively as well as true and sober. There will be no hypocritical exposure or little religious games of make-believe.

Unfortunately, some become inflated both inwardly and outwardly. They prop themselves up with words that imply humility and gesture with signs of devotion. They want to appear holy in our sight, rather than holy in God's sight. They work hard at it. Ah, Lord God! Humble mannerisms reveal a proud heart. The truly humble speak and gesture with reserve. Our words and outward gestures need to reflect an inner humility. Speak in a normal, natural voice. If the words are true, utter them in a truthful way.

What more do I need to say about these toxic self-deceptions? I honestly think that unless we have the good judgment to avoid such whining hypocrisy, which links the secret pride in the heart with spoken words and actions, we will soon sink down into sorrow.

CHAPTER 55

Condemning others

The fiendish devil has yet another way to deceive us. Amazingly, he inspires people to uphold God's law and to destroy sin in others. Instead of tempting them with something that is clearly evil, he sets them to work like busy prelates, screening every detail of their Christian living. They act like an abbot overseeing his monks. Assuming pastoral care, they point out flaws in everyone. They criticize everyone, claiming that a burning love of God in their hearts motivates them. Instead, the fire of hell, burning in their brains and imaginations, prompts this activity.

The devil is spiritual in nature and does not possess a body any more than an angel does. When he, or an angel, would take bodily form (with God's permission) to do some work in this world, the type of body assumed corresponds to the nature of the work. Holy Scripture gives us an example of this. The Old and New Testaments always report that when an angel was sent in bodily form, there was something about it, in name or character, that revealed its function and message. The same is true of the devil. When he appears in human form, some quality of his body will mirror his intention.

One instance of this will stand for many. Those who delve in necromancy, who study the calling up of wicked spirits, have sometimes seen the devil appear in bodily form. They tell me that he always has one nostril, widely open. He wants his victims to look all the way up his nose to his brain, which is nothing other than hellfire. If he can get someone to look into the hellish flames, that individual will lose his mind forever. A trained student of necromancy knows this, and he keeps things under control and takes steps to avoid harm.

Whenever the devil takes on a body, it will reflect his business. In relation to the religious enthusiasm we have been discussing, he inflames the imagination of his contemplatives with the fire of hell, igniting weird ideas. Without any justification, they accept it as their responsibility to censure and admonish others. They do this because they have only one spiritual nostril.

Our noses are divided into two nostrils, suggesting that we should be able to distinguish good from evil, evil from worse evil, and the good from the better, before we begin passing judgment on what we have heard or seen.

CHAPTER 56
Common sense and common doctrine

The devil's illusions do not deceive everyone, but some who escape still discard the common doctrine of the Christian church. They take pride in their intellectual curiosity and education. They depend too much on their acquired knowledge. Because they never received a foundation of meek, blind feeling, or virtuous living, they are subject to false feelings and delusions. They go to the extreme of saying bad things about the saints, the sacraments, and the ordinances of the Holy Church. Worldly people consider church rules too difficult to follow. They look for an easier way than the one ordained by the church.

If you will not travel the challenging and narrow road to heaven, you will follow the easy path to hell. We will witness this separation on the last day. I believe that if we could see heretics and their followers as they will be seen on judgment day, we would know that their lives are infested with secret sin, in addition to their open teaching of error. We could call them disciples of the Antichrist. They display virtue in public, but in private, they are lustful lechers.

CHAPTER 57

Presumptuous beginners

I have digressed. Let's return now to my discussion of young and presumptuous spiritual disciples who misunderstand the use of language.

When they hear "lift up your hearts to God," they begin to look up at the stars as though they were trying to reach beyond the moon, and listen intently for the music of heavenly angels. Sometimes they imagine they have soared into heaven, opening a hole in the firmament in order to look for God. Their fantasy creates a God to fit their preconceived notions, clothing him in royal garments and setting him upon an ornate throne. They imagine angels in human form gathered around God, like an orchestra on a stage before a conductor. They "see" and report all of this in meticulous detail. The devil deceives them in remarkable ways. When dew falls, they think it is the food of angels drifting through the air and making a sweet taste in their mouths. This explains why they sit with gaping mouths as though they were catching flies.

This may seem holy, but it is pure deception. Their souls are empty of true devotion. Vanity and falsehood overtake them because they are contemplating in the wrong way. Yes, the devil's trickery supplies strange sounds, lights, and odors.

These beginners do not recognize the truth about their experiences. They think looking upward emulates St. Martin, who saw God wrapped in a cloak among his angels, or St. Stephen, who saw our Lord standing in heaven. They claim the example of Christ, who ascended bodily into heaven. This is why they look up.

I agree that we should lift up our eyes and our hands if the Spirit moves us, but we are not to direct our spiritual efforts up or down, to one side or the other, forward or backward. Contemplative prayer has no spatial orientation. We are not to contemplate in a physical manner.

CHAPTER 58

Forcing imagination

Consider what we hear about St. Martin and St. Stephen. Even if they saw those things with their physical eyes, God miraculously disclosed the visions to them for spiritual assurance. Christ had no need of St. Martin's cloak in order to keep warm. The vision is a symbolic miracle that assures us we are capable of receiving salvation and becoming spiritually united with the body of Christ. When we give clothing to the poor or perform other good deeds for the love of God, spiritually or physically, it will be as though they are done to Christ's own body. He tells us that in the Gospel.

Christ did not think it was enough to just speak the words about this. He affirmed what he had said by revealing himself miraculously to St. Martin. All spiritual visions have spiritual meaning. I believe that if people who report them had enough depth of spirituality, they would have been able to perceive their significance without requiring God to display them in physical form. Discard the shell and eat the sweet kernel.

How? Not in the manner of the heretics who behave like crazy people, throwing their cups against the wall and breaking them as soon as they have had a drink. Do not eat the fruit in a way that will make you despise the tree. The cup and the tree are visible miracles, and those bodily gestures that are in harmony with the spirit do not hinder spiritual work. If we do these things because the Spirit moves us, then they are well done. If not, they are hypocrisy and lies. If they are true and contain spiritual fruit, we need not despise them. We may kiss the cup because of the wine it contains.

How shall we interpret our Lord's physical ascension into heaven while his mother and his disciples watched? Does this mean we should stare toward the sky when we do our spiritual exercises, trying to see him sitting in heaven or standing as St. Stephen saw him? Of course not. His revelation to St. Stephen does not instruct us to look up toward heaven physically when we do our spiritual work, in order to see him standing, sitting, or lying down there. We do not understand the nature of Christ's resurrected body and should not imagine him taking various positions. All we need to know is that his body and soul are united eternally in divine glory. His humanity and his divinity are one.

If Christ would show himself as sitting, standing, or lying down to anyone living in this world, his intention would be to convey a spiritual message. His posture would not be important.

Standing, though, we can interpret as supportive. We say to our friends, "Stand up to it! Fight against your difficulties. I will stand by you." This does not mean simply standing there physically, but that we are ready to help. The person we speak to might be engaged in battle and seated on horseback at the time. This explains why our Lord showed himself as standing to St. Stephen as Christ's foes martyred him by stoning. He did not grant the vision to teach us to look up to heaven.

Christ revealed himself to St. Stephen in this way because he knew others would also suffer persecution for his love.

He is assuring all of us that he will stand by us in all the power of his godliness when we are persecuted for his sake. He encourages us to be brave. Spiritual meaning prompts all of Christ's bodily appearances.

CHAPTER 59
Time, place, and prayer

Regarding the Ascension of our Lord, you should not think of it as a physical performance with a spiritual meaning. He had been dead. At the time of the Ascension, he was clothed in his immortal *resurrected* body, as we shall be on Judgment Day. We will experience a freedom of motion similar to what we can accomplish with our imaginations now. Spatial dimensions will not limit us. Remember that we will not enter heaven physically, but only spiritually. Heaven has nothing physical about it, neither up nor down, right nor left, forward nor backward.

If you attempt to follow the instructions of this book, fully understand that although you may read "lift up" or "go in" or "stirring," these terms have nothing at all to do with physical relationships. The stirrings I describe do not move you from one place to another. If I tell you about "rest," do not think of it as the kind of rest you can have in a bed or a chair. At its best, contemplation is purely spiritual, involving something far different from physically stirring from one place to another.

Perhaps it would be better to speak of it as a sudden "changing" rather than as a stirring. Forget about time, place, and body when you engage in spiritual effort. Do not misinterpret the Ascension of Christ in a way that strains your imagination when you pray. Do not try to move upward as though you want to climb over the moon. This is not the way to pray.

You are not God. Ascending into heaven the way Christ did, Jesus himself assures us in the Gospel of John, is impossible for us. He is the only one capable of such an ascent. Anyway, when Christ ascended into heaven it was an achievement of great spiritual power, and not imaginative straining. Avoid erroneous spiritual illusions.

CHAPTER 60
Desire

You remain puzzled. You naturally think of heaven as "up." The ascension of Christ seems to confirm this spatial relationship. The Holy Spirit descends "from above." We believe the disciples saw these things happen. You think Scripture provides all the evidence you need to prove that you should direct your mind physically upward when you pray.

As humbly as I can, I will answer this way: Since Christ ascended and then sent the Holy Spirit, it was natural that it be upward and from above, rather than downward and from beneath, or behind, or before, or on one side or the other. But the spatial references are only symbolic. He had no need to move in one direction or the other. The spiritual realm is always near, enveloping us on every side.

Whoever has a strong desire to be in heaven is already in heaven, spiritually. Measure the highway to heaven in terms of desire rather than miles. This is what St. Paul means when he says that even though our bodies are earthbound now, our living is in heaven. He writes of spiritual love and desire. Love determines a soul's location. If you want to go to heaven spiritually, there is no need to strain up or down, or to one side or the other.

CHAPTER 61

Spirit and flesh

If our spirit prompt us, we may lift our eyes and our hands physically toward the sky. The spirit controls our gestures. Physical things depend upon spiritual things, and not the opposite.

Look again at the Ascension of our Lord. When the proper time had come for him to return to his Father in heaven, then the tremendous power of his divine Spirit swept him up as a unified person.

Those who attempt the spiritual work described in this book will experience the same subjection of the body to the spirit. Good prayer results in good posture. Without noticing it, we will stand more erect by the power of the spirit. God made us so that our faces look up toward the sky rather than down at the earth like beasts. You may see our noble spiritual destiny in the fact that God designed us to reach out spiritually toward him.

Be careful, then, not to interpret spiritual things in physical terms. While we must communicate with the vocabulary of regular human speech, this does not mean that we must always take the language literally. We are able to go beyond the simple meaning of words and grasp their spiritual significance.

CHAPTER 62
Understanding spiritual activity

To assist your spiritual understanding of ordinary language, I will explain the terminology we use. This may help spare you some basic mistakes.

The created universe is all around you. The sun, moon, and stars are external. They are above you, but at the same time, they are beneath your soul. That is to say, they are splendid, but your human dignity is even more splendid.

Your soul has three primary powers:
- Mind
- Reason
- Will

There are two secondary powers:
- Imagination
- Sensuality

God alone is above you in nature.

When you see the word "yourself" in devotional books, understand that it means your soul and not your body. Evaluate the quality of your achievements according to the working of your soul. Then you will know if your work is beneath you, within you, or above you.

CHAPTER 63

Mind

Our minds do not work independently of our other faculties. The mind collects, sorts, and remembers information variously received. The mind, then, is different in nature from reason, will, imagination, and sensuality. Its job is to comprehend.

I label some of the powers of the soul "primary" and some "secondary." We cannot compartmentalize the soul, but we may categorize the information it digests. I list spiritual things as primary, and material things as secondary. The two working primary powers, reason and will, deal directly with spiritual matters, functioning independently of imagination and sensuality. The latter perform using the body's senses in the same manner as animals. Without assistance from reason and will, it is not possible for the soul to understand the nature of physical creatures, nor the source of their creation. This explains why I call reason and will primary powers. They function entirely in the spiritual dimension. I designate imagination and sensuality secondary powers because they are bodily functions of our five senses. I label mind a primary power because it contains the other powers, as well as the information they absorb. I will explain this in more detail.

CHAPTER 64

Reason and will

Reason permits us to determine the difference between good and evil, bad from worse, good from better, worse from the worst, and better from the best. Before Adam's sin in the Garden of Eden, reason performed all of this naturally. Now, original sin blinds reason, and it is likely to make mistakes unless God's grace grants illumination. The mind contains and understands both reason and the object upon which it works.

We use our wills to choose the good that reason points out to us. We *will* to love the good, we desire the good, and we consent to be in God. Before Adam's fall, the will could make no bad choices. Human will naturally knew what was good and loved it. That is not possible now, unless it has received God's grace. The infection of original sin makes us perceive something evil as good.

CHAPTER 65
Imagination

Imagination allows us to depict for ourselves the images of absent and present things. Both the imagination and the images it produces are in the mind. Before Adam's sin, imagination obeyed reason and was reason's servant. Twisted notions of physical or spiritual things never deceived reason. Because of our fall from grace, imagination never stops twisting the information it receives from the material world, and it invents fantasies of spiritual things. Unless God's grace restrains it, we fall into great error.

We may easily observe this disobedience of the imagination in the approach to prayer by newly converted individuals. Until the light of grace restrains the imagination, which results from constant meditation on spiritual topics for an extended time, these new converts are not able to control the amazing thoughts, fantasies, and images that make strong impressions on their minds. All of this is a product of original sin.

CHAPTER 66
Sensuality

The soul's power of sensuality allows us to feel things through our senses. This ability lets us know and experience material things, deciding which is pleasant and which is harmful. Sensuality has two aspects. Externally, it tends to the needs of the body. Internally, it enjoys pleasure.

Sensuality complains when the body does not get the sustenance that it needs. When it notices special requirements, sensuality urges us to take more than we need, encouraging lust. It complains when pleasant sensations are not experienced, and is delighted when they are. Sensuality protests irritation and welcomes the absence of pain. This power and its functioning are in the mind.

Before Adam's fall, sensuality was subservient to the will. Improper pleasure and annoyance with physical things or spiritual expression did not exist. Now things have changed.

Unless God's grace in the will controls sensuality, allowing it to endure humbly the deprivations of original sin, lustful pleasure will dominate. Sensuality will wallow like a hog in the mire among the wealth and flesh of this world, leading our lives to become more beastly and carnal than human and spiritual.

CHAPTER 67

The spiritual way

I have shown you, my friend, the wretchedness of our condition as fallen creatures warped by original sin. Blind, we easily misunderstand the meaning of spiritual language, misapplying spiritual activities. Many of us are ignorant of spiritual power and do not understand how the soul functions.

If your mind becomes preoccupied with material things, regardless of how good they might be, you are beneath yourself, outside your soul.

If you become aware that your mind occupies itself with the intricacies of the soul and the way things work in spiritual matters, then you are within yourself and on the way toward spiritual perfection.

If your mind occupies itself with nothing material and nothing spiritual other than God alone, as the practice taught in this book may permit, then you are above yourself and under God.

Why do I say you are "above yourself"? I say it because when this happens, you have reached by grace a condition you cannot reach by nature. You are spiritually united with God in love, and in harmony with his will. You are "under God," because even though you are one in spirit, you remain beneath him. God exists from all eternity, and you are his creation. Your union is a gift from God. You may be one with God and yet remain far beneath the nature of God.

You can see, then, that if you are ignorant of the powers of your own soul, and of the manner in which these powers function, you can easily think erroneously when you read spiritual literature. You can also see, my friend, why I refrained from encouraging you to reveal your desire to God, but asked you to try to hide it like a child. I did not want you to understand spiritual ideas in common, literal ways.

CHAPTER 68

Nowhere is everywhere

If someone were to tell you to collect all your abilities within yourself and worship God there, I would object. I am concerned that you might misinterpret these well-spoken words. They are true if you understand them properly. The risk is that you might accept them in a physical way. Be careful that you are in no sense "within yourself." I am asking you not to think in terms of being anywhere. Do not be inside yourself, outside yourself, above yourself, behind yourself, or on one side or the other.

You are puzzled and ask, "Then where am I to be? Nowhere?" Yes! You've got it! Nowhere bodily is everywhere spiritually. Make your spiritual exercise nowhere. If you do this, you will be with God in spirit as truly as your body is located at a spot on earth. This results in an enormous advantage. Your physical facilities will not be able to find anything to stimulate them. It will seem to them that you are doing nothing. Wonderful! Continue doing that nothing, as long as you are doing it for the love of God. Do not stop. Work hard at it with a powerful desire to be with an unknowable God.

I prefer to be "nowhere" physically like this, wrestling with that blind "nothingness," than to be rich enough to go anywhere I want on earth and play with any of its "somethings."

Forget this "everywhere" and these "somethings"; choose "nowhere" and this "nothingness." Do not worry if you are not able to figure this out in your mind. That is the way it is supposed to be. This nothingness lies beyond your grasp. It can be felt more easily than seen. It envelopes those who contemplate it even briefly in blinding darkness. An abundance of spiritual light creates this darkness. Only our outward nature calls it "nothing." Our inner nature calls it "All." It teaches the essence of all things, both physical and spiritual, without giving specific attention to any one thing alone.

CHAPTER 69

Nothingness and love

The experience of this "nothing" that happens "nowhere" dramatically transforms our love. The instant we look at it, we see hidden images of every sin we have committed since childhood. Our sins unavoidably remain before us until we have rubbed them away with groans and bitter tears.

Sometimes we even feel like we are looking into hell. We wonder if we will ever reach our goal of the peace of spiritual perfection while enduring such grief and pain. This frightens some away. They are not able to endure the distress until spiritual consolation arrives.

If you continue contemplation, you will eventually experience some pleasure and encouragement. You will perceive that God's grace has wiped away many sins that you have committed. The pain will persist, but will gradually diminish until you realize it will end. Rather than hell, it becomes purgatory.

Sometimes, no particular sin comes forward. You will understand that sin is an indefinable lump that is nothing other than yourself, the painful root of original sin. At other times, the experience will seem like paradise or heaven because of the many wonderful sweet pleasures, joys, and blessed virtues that you discover. Sometimes there will be so much peace and repose in that darkness that you will think you must be in God's holy presence.

You may formulate many interpretations of this nothingness, but ultimately, you will always understand that it is a thick *cloud of unknowing* that is between you and God.

CHAPTER 70

Comprehending God

Continue working, then, in this nothing and in this nowhere, turning away from your outward physical senses and their stimulants. I emphasize that sensuality will never comprehend God. God designed your eyes to observe the size, shape, color, and position of physical objects. Sound waves stimulate your ears. Your nose smells the difference between good and bad odors. Your tongue tastes sweet and sour, salt and fresh, pleasant and bitter. Your sense of touch informs you of hot and cold, hard and soft, smooth and sharp. Neither God nor spiritual things have any of these qualities.

Therefore, do not use your outward senses in any way. When contemplatives want to hear, smell, see, taste, or touch spiritual things, either within or beyond themselves, they are mistaken. This is the wrong approach. Nature directs that our bodily senses should perceive physical things rather than spiritual things. We gain knowledge of spiritual things without the use of our senses.

God remains far beyond even our most profound spiritual understanding. We will know God when spiritual understanding fails, because God is where it breaks down. St. Denis wrote, "The only divine knowledge of God is that which is known by unknowing." If you read the work of St. Denis, you will find agreement with the things I am telling you in this book. I will not quote other passages from his or any other work. Writers used to think that humility required them to say nothing out of their own heads, but to corroborate every idea with quotations from Scripture or the fathers. Today, this practice demonstrates nothing but cleverness and education. I am not going to do it because you do not need it. Christ said, "He who has ears, let him hear." If God moves you to believe what I say, then accept my ideas on their own merits.

CHAPTER 71

Variety of experience

Some people believe that contemplation is too difficult and awesome. They think it requires difficult preparation and that it rarely happens except during a moment of rapture. I will attempt to answer them the best I can.

Success depends upon two things: the gift of God and the spiritual capacity of the one contemplating. Some require long and difficult preparation. For these, it will be a rare occurrence, a moment of rapture especially given by God.

But others are more naturally inclined and more familiar with God. They may experience divine contemplation at surprising times in an ordinary state of soul. They retain complete control of all of their faculties and can continue using them if they wish.

Moses is an example of the first type, and his brother, Aaron, the temple priest, is the other. The Old Testament ark of the covenant represents the grace of contemplation. Those who were most involved with caring for the ark are contemplative souls. The ark is like the gift of contemplation because it contains all the jewels and treasures of the temple. Love that is intent on God in the *cloud of unknowing* contains all the virtues of the soul, which is the spiritual temple of God.

Before the ark of the covenant existed, Moses climbed to the top of the mountain, camped up there, and labored in a cloud for six days. On the seventh day, our Lord showed him how to construct the ark of the covenant. The long labor of

Moses and the tardy disclosure he received represent the ones who do not arrive at perfection in this spiritual effort without extended effort. Success comes only when God allows it.

Moses rarely visited the ark of the covenant. Aaron worked in the temple and could see the ark behind its veil whenever he wished. Aaron represents those who easily and frequently achieve contemplative perfection because they have spiritual awareness and God's grace assists them.

CHAPTER 72

Differences

People are different. We must not judge others in terms of our own experience, or expect them to contemplate exactly as we do. Whether we are like Moses or like Aaron, we must not assume everyone should be like us. If it is God's pleasure, change can affect all of us, and our circumstances can be reversed.

CHAPTER 73

Contributions

The Old Testament tells us three men were involved with the ark of the covenant: Moses, Aaron, and Bezalel. Bezalel was the artisan who constructed the ark in the valley after Moses came down from the mountain with its design.

These three represent three approaches to contemplation. Sometimes we must climb the mountain and trust God's grace, like Moses. Moses worked hard at his task, but God's rare revelation to Moses was a gift and not a reward that he had earned.

Sometimes our own spiritual acuity, working together with grace, brings progress in contemplation. Then we are like Bezalel, who needed the pattern Moses received on the mountain and could not conceive the ark himself before he skillfully constructed it.

Sometimes we progress when grace reaches us through the teaching of others. Then we are like Aaron. While he neither conceived of the ark of the covenant nor constructed it, he took care of it.

So, my spiritual friend, I may be unworthy and a poor teacher. I am in Bezalel's position. My purpose is to make a spiritual ark, describing its nature and showing you how to use your hands to construct it. Your work can be much better and more valuable than mine, if you will be as Aaron, continually working in this for both you and me. Do this, I pray, for the love of God. God has called both of us to do this work. I beg you, for the love of God, to add your own ability to mine, making up for my inadequacy.

CHAPTER 74

Recognition

If, after reading this book, you think my approach to divine contemplation is not your style, then abandon it. Seek another way, more suited for your personal needs. There is no risk, and I will not reproach you as long as you seek good spiritual direction. In such a case, please excuse me. Honestly, my purpose in writing this book was to help you make progress along the lines of my own simple experience. Read the book over two or three times before you decide. The more you read this book, the more you will understand it. If a particular sentence seems hard to follow the first or second time you read it, you may easily understand it on the third reading.

I think it is impossible that anyone with an inclination to contemplation could read this book, privately or aloud, without experiencing a positive attraction to what I am saying. If you think this book is doing you good, thank God, and for the love of God, pray for me.

I also ask you, for the love of God, not to let anyone examine this book except those who might respond to it positively. I mentioned this at the beginning. If you pass this along to someone else, give him or her the time to digest it. No one should flip through its pages, reading a little here and a little there. Let your friend read from cover to cover. Perhaps a question occurs at the beginning or in the middle that is not fully explained right then, but will be later on. Whoever reads one section and not the others could easily fall into error. I plead with you to do as I say. If you think there is anything in this book that needs clarification, let me know what it is and what you think about it. I will improve it the best I can with my simple ability.

As for the chatterboxes, the rumormongers, the gossips, the tattletales, and the faultfinders of every kind, I do not want them to see this book. I never intended to write on this subject for them, and I do not want them tampering with it. This also applies to clever clerics and lay people. Regardless of their good involvement in the active life, what I have to say here is not for them.

CHAPTER 75

Certainty

All who read this book, or listen to it read aloud, and feel a resonant response, should not necessarily feel called by God to begin this exercise. Congenial feeling may result from natural intellectual curiosity rather than a calling of God's grace.

If you want to be sure of the source of your feeling, there is a way you can test it. Have you done everything possible to prepare yourself by cleansing your conscience according to church practice, and with the guidance of a spiritual director? Good! If you want to know more, ask yourself whether this desire is pressing on you more constantly than any other spiritual exercise. If it seems to you that nothing you do, physically or spiritually, is of much value other than this little secret love, then you have a call from God.

I do not say that the ones God calls to contemplation will continuously feel this stirring in their minds. No, it does not work that way. In fact, sometimes God withdraws an attraction to this work from young spiritual disciples. This prevents the presumption that it was the result of one's own ability to contemplate whenever he or she desires. When God's grace is withdrawn, pride is usually the culprit. I mean, withdrawn grace prevents pride. Often young people foolishly think God is their enemy when he is their best friend.

Carelessness also interferes with this experience and causes painful withdrawing. Sometimes our Lord intentionally delays the experience, intending to enlarge it and make it more valuable when it returns. Here is one of the best ways you can tell whether God is calling you to this exercise: Do you feel, after a delay and long absence of this experience, when it suddenly returns without any special effort on your part, that you have a greater stirring of desire and a greater longing to contemplate God than ever before? A simple indicator is that your joy is greater when you rediscover it than your sorrow was when you lost it. If it works this way for you, then you have an authentic token that God calls you to the contemplative life, regardless of your past.

The important consideration is not what you are, or what you have been, but what you want to be. This is what matters to a merciful God. St. Gregory said, "All holy desires grow by delay. If they diminish when delayed they were not holy desires." If you rejoice in new discoveries and unexpected answers to old prayers, then, even though they may have been natural desires with good intentions, they were never holy desires. St. Augustine said, "The whole life of good Christians is nothing other than holy desires."

Farewell, spiritual friend. Go with God's blessing and mine. I pray that God will give you true peace, sensible guidance, and spiritual comfort. May God's grace always be with you, and with all those on earth who love God. Amen.

APPENDIX

EDITOR'S NOTE

Evelyn Underhill helped awaken interest in Christian spiritual classics during the early years of the twentieth century. Her contagious enthusiasm for widely neglected books led a generation into a rediscovery of the literary treasures of the church. She encouraged John M. Watkins to modernize one of the six manuscripts of *The Cloud of Unknowing* preserved by the British Museum. An earlier attempt, in 1871, by Henry Collins was distressingly inadequate. "The pithy sayings of the original are either misquoted, or expanded into conventional and flavorless sentences. Numerous explanatory phrases for which our manuscripts give no authority have been incorporated into the text. All the quaint and humorous turns of speech are omitted or toned down." Published in 1922, the new rendering included an informed introduction by Underhill. Because of its value, her essay is included here for modern readers. Her quotations from *The Cloud* are from the version prepared by Watkins.

ESSAY ON *THE CLOUD OF UNKNOWING*
by Evelyn Underhill

The little family of mystical treatises which is known to students as "the Cloud of Unknowing group," deserves more attention than it has hitherto received from English lovers of mysticism: for it represents the first expression in our own tongue of that great mystic tradition of the Christian Neoplatonists which gathered up, remade, and "salted with Christ's salt" all that was best in the spiritual wisdom of the ancient world.

That wisdom made its definite entrance into the Catholic fold about AD 500, in the writings of the profound and nameless mystic who chose to call himself "Dionysius the Areopagite." Three hundred and fifty years later, those writings were translated into Latin by John Scotus Erigena, a scholar at the court of Charlemagne, and so became available to the ecclesiastical world of the West. Another five hundred years elapsed, during which their influence was felt, and felt strongly, by the mystics of every European country: by St. Bernard, the Victorines, St. Bonaventura, St. Thomas Aquinas. Every reader of Dante knows the part which they play in the *Paradiso*. Then, about the middle of the fourteenth century, England—at that time in the height of her great mystical period—led the way with the first translation into the vernacular of the Areopagite's work. In *Dionise Hid Divinite*, a version of the *Mystica Theologia*, this spiritual treasure-house was first made accessible to those outside the professionally religious class. Surely this is a fact which all lovers of mysticism, all "spiritual patriots," should be concerned to hold in remembrance.

It is supposed by most scholars that *Dionise Hid Divinite*, which—appearing as it did in an epoch of great spiritual vitality—quickly attained to a considerable circulation, is by the same hand which wrote the *Cloud of Unknowing* and its companion books; and that this hand also produced an English paraphrase of Richard of St. Victor's *Benjamin Minor*, another work of much authority on the contemplative life. Certainly the influence of Richard is only second to that of Dionysius in this unknown mystic's own work—work, however, which owes as much to the deep personal experience, and extraordinary psychological gifts of its writer, as to the tradition that he inherited from the past.

Nothing is known of him; beyond the fact, which seems clear from his writings, that he was a cloistered monk devoted to the contemplative life. It has been thought that he was a Carthusian. But the rule of that austere order, whose members live in hermit-like seclusion, and scarcely meet except for the purpose of divine worship, can hardly have afforded him opportunity of observing and enduring all those tiresome tricks and absurd mannerisms of which he gives so amusing and realistic a description in the lighter passages of the *Cloud*. These passages betray the half-humorous exasperation of the temperamental recluse, nervous, fastidious, and hypersensitive, loving silence and peace, but compelled to a daily and hourly companionship with persons of a less contemplative type: some finding in extravagant and meaningless gestures an outlet for suppressed vitality; others overflowing with a terrible cheerfulness like "giggling girls and nice japing jugglers"; others so lacking in repose that they "can neither sit still, stand still, nor lie still, unless they be either wagging with their feet or else somewhat doing with their hands." Though he cannot go to the length of condemning these habits as mortal sins, the author of the *Cloud* leaves us in no doubt as to the irritation with which they inspired him, or the distrust with which he regards the spiritual claims of those who fidget.

The attempt to identify this mysterious writer with Walter Hilton, the author of *The Scale of Perfection*, has completely failed: though Hilton's work—especially the exquisite fragment called the *Song of Angels*—certainly betrays his influence. The works attributed to him, if we exclude the translations from Dionysius and Richard of St. Victor, are only five in number. They are, first, *The Cloud of Unknowing*—the longest and most complete exposition of its author's peculiar doctrine—and, depending from it, four short tracts or letters: *The Epistle of Prayer, The Epistle of Discretion in the Stirrings of the Soul, The Epistle of Privy Counsel*, and *The Treatise of Discerning of Spirits*. Some critics have even disputed the claim of the writer of the *Cloud* to the authorship of these little works, regarding them as the production of a group or school of contemplatives devoted to the study and practice of the Dionysian mystical theology; but the unity of thought and style found in them makes this hypothesis at least improbable. Everything points rather to their being the work of an original mystical genius, of strongly marked character and great literary ability: who, whilst he took the framework of his philosophy from Dionysius the Areopagite, and of his psychology from Richard of St. Victor, yet is in no sense a mere imitator of these masters, but introduced a genuinely new element into mediaeval religious literature.

What, then, were his special characteristics? Whence came the fresh color which he gave to the old Platonic theory of mystical experience? First, I think, from the combination of high spiritual gifts with a vivid sense of humor, keen powers of observation, a robust common-sense: a balance of qualities not indeed rare amongst the mystics, but here presented to us in an extreme form. In his eager gazing on divinity this contemplative never loses touch with humanity, never forgets the sovereign purpose of his writings; which is not a declaration of the spiritual favors he has received, but a helping of his fellow-men to share them. Next, he has a great simplicity of outlook, which enables him to present the result of his highest experiences and intuitions in the most direct and homely language. So actual, and so much a part of his normal existence, are his apprehensions of spiritual reality, that he can give them to us in the plain words of daily life: and thus he is one of the most realistic of mystical writers. He abounds in vivid little phrases—"Call sin a *lump*": "Short prayer pierceth heaven": "Nowhere bodily, is everywhere ghostly": "Who that will not go the strait way to heaven, . . . shall go the soft way to hell." His range of experience is a wide one. He does not disdain to take a hint from the wizards and necromancers on the right way to treat the devil; he draws his illustrations of divine mercy from the homeliest incidents of friendship and parental love. A skilled theologian, quoting St. Augustine and Thomas Aquinas, and using with ease the language of scholasticism, he is able, on the other hand, to express the deepest speculations of mystical philosophy without resorting to academic terminology: as for instance where he describes the spiritual heaven as a "state" rather than a "place":

"For heaven ghostly is as nigh down as up, and up as down: behind as before, before as behind, on one side as other. Insomuch, that whoso had a true desire for to be at heaven, then that same time he were in heaven ghostly. For the high and the next way thither is run by desires, and not by paces of feet."

His writings, though they touch on many subjects, are chiefly concerned with the art of contemplative prayer; that "blind intent stretching to God" which, if it be wholly set on Him, cannot fail to reach its goal. A peculiar talent for the description and discrimination of spiritual states has enabled him to discern and set before us, with astonishing precision and vividness, not only the strange sensations, the confusion and bewilderment of the beginner in the early stages of contemplation—the struggle with distracting thoughts, the silence, the dark—and the unfortunate state of those theoretical mystics who, "swollen with pride and with curiosity of much clergy and letterly cunning as in clerks," miss that treasure which is "never got by study but all only by grace"; but also the happiness of those whose "sharp dart of longing love" has not "failed of the prick, the which is God."

A great simplicity characterizes his doctrine of the soul's attainment of the Absolute. For him there is but one central necessity: the perfect and passionate setting of the will upon the Divine, so that it is "thy love and thy meaning, the choice and point of thine heart." Not by deliberate ascetic practices, not by refusal of the world, not by intellectual striving, but by actively loving and choosing, by that which a modern psychologist has called "the synthesis of love and will" does the spirit of man achieve its goal. "For silence is not God," he says in the *Epistle of Discretion*, "nor speaking is not God; fasting is not God, nor eating is not God; loneliness is not God, nor company is not God; nor yet any of all the other two such contraries. He is hid between them, and may not be found by any work of thy soul, but all only by love of thine heart. He may not be known by reason, He may not be gotten by thought, nor concluded by understanding; but He may be loved and chosen with the true lovely will of thine heart. . . . Such a blind shot with the sharp dart of longing love may never fail of the prick, the which is God."

To him who has so loved and chosen, and "in a true will and by an whole intent does purpose him to be a perfect follower of Christ, not only in active living, but in the sovereignest point of contemplative living, the which is possible by grace for to be come to in this present life," these writings are addressed. In the prologue of *The Cloud of Unknowing* we find the warning, so often prefixed to mediaeval mystical works, that it shall on no account be lent, given, or read to other men: who could not understand, and might misunderstand in a dangerous sense, its peculiar message. Nor was this warning a mere expression of literary vanity. If we may judge by the examples of possible misunderstanding against which he is careful to guard himself, the almost tiresome reminders that all his remarks are "ghostly, not bodily meant," the standard of intelligence which the author expected from his readers was not a high one. He even fears that some "young presumptuous ghostly disciples" may understand the injunction to "lift up the heart" in a merely physical manner; and either "stare in the stars as if they would be above the moon," or "travail their fleshly hearts outrageously in their breasts" in the effort to make literal "ascensions" to God. Eccentricities of this kind he finds not only foolish but dangerous; they outrage nature, destroy sanity and health, and "hurt full sore the silly soul, and make it fester in fantasy feigned of fiends." He observes with a touch of arrogance that his book is not intended for these undisciplined seekers after the abnormal and the marvelous, nor yet for "fleshly janglers, flatterers and blamers, . . . nor none of these curious, lettered, nor unlearned men." It is to those who feel themselves called to the true prayer of contemplation, to the search for God, whether in the cloister or the world—whose "little secret love" is at once the energizing cause of all action, and the hidden sweet savor of life—that he addresses himself. These he instructs in that simple yet difficult art of recollection, the necessary preliminary of any true communion with the spiritual order, in which all sensual images, all memories and thoughts, are as he says, "trodden down under the cloud of forgetting" until "nothing lives in the working mind but a naked intent stretching to God." This "intent stretching"—this loving and vigorous determination of the will—he regards as the central fact of the mystical life; the very heart of effective prayer. Only by its exercise can the spirit, freed from the distractions of memory and sense, focus itself upon Reality and ascend with "a privy love pressed" to that "Cloud of Unknowing"—the Divine Ignorance of the Neoplatonists—wherein is "knit up the ghostly knot of burning love betwixt thee and thy God, in ghostly onehead and according of will."

There is in this doctrine something which should be peculiarly congenial to the activistic tendencies of modern thought. Here is no taint of quietism, no invitation to a spiritual limpness. From first to last glad and deliberate work is demanded of the initiate: an all-round wholeness of experience is insisted on. "A man may not be fully active, but if he be in part contemplative; nor yet fully contemplative, as it may be here, but if he be in part active." Over and over again, the emphasis is laid on this active aspect of all true spirituality—always a favorite theme of the great English mystics. "Love cannot be lazy," said Richard Rolle. So too for the author of the *Cloud* energy is the mark of true affection. "Do forth ever, more and more, so that thou be ever doing. . . . Do on then fast; let see how thou bearest thee. Seest thou not how He standeth and abideth thee?"

True, the will alone, however ardent and industrious, cannot of itself set up communion with the supernal world: this is "the work of only God, specially wrought in what soul that Him liketh." But man can and must do his part. First, there are the virtues to be acquired: those "ornaments of the Spiritual Marriage" with which no mystic can dispense. Since we can but behold that which we are, his character must be set in order, his mind and heart made beautiful and pure, before he can look on the triple star of Goodness, Truth, and Beauty, which is God. Every great spiritual teacher has spoken in the same sense: of the need for that which Rolle calls the "mending of life"—regeneration, the rebuilding of character—as the preparation of the contemplative act.

For the author of the *Cloud* all human virtue is comprised in the twin qualities of Humility and Charity. He who has these, has all. Humility, in accordance with the doctrine of Richard of St. Victor, he identifies with self-knowledge; the terrible vision of the soul as it is, which induces first self-abasement and then self-purification—the beginning of all spiritual growth, and the necessary antecedent of all knowledge of God. "Therefore swink and sweat in all that thou canst and mayst, for to get thee a true knowing and a feeling of thyself as thou art; and then I troy that soon after that, thou shalt have a true knowing and a feeling of God as He is."

As all man's feeling and thought of himself and his relation to God is comprehended in Humility, so all his feeling and thought of God in Himself is comprehended in Charity; the self-giving love of Divine Perfection "in Himself and for Himself" which Hilton calls "the sovereign and the essential joy." Together these two virtues should embrace the sum of his responses to the Universe; they should govern his attitude to man as well as his attitude to God. "Charity is nought else . . . but love of God for Himself above all creatures, and of man for God even as thyself."

Charity and Humility, then, together with the ardent and industrious will, are the necessary possessions of each soul set upon this adventure. Their presence it is which marks out the true from the false mystic: and it would seem, from the detailed, vivid, and often amusing descriptions of the sanctimonious, the hypocritical, the self-sufficient, and the self-deceived in their "diverse and wonderful variations," that such a test was as greatly needed in the "Ages of Faith" as it is at the present day. Sham spirituality flourished in the mediaeval cloister, and offered a constant opportunity of error to those young enthusiasts who were not yet aware that the true freedom of eternity "cometh not with observation." Affectations of sanctity, pretense to rare mystical experiences, were a favorite means of advertisement. Psychic phenomena, too, seem to have been common: ecstasies, visions, voices, the scent of strange perfumes, the hearing of sweet sounds. For these supposed indications of Divine favor, the author of the *Cloud* has no more respect than the modern psychologist: and here, of course, he is in agreement with all the greatest writers on mysticism, who are unanimous in their dislike and distrust of all visionary and auditory experience. Such things, he considers, are most often hallucination: and, where they are not, should be regarded as the accidents rather than the substance of the contemplative life—the harsh rind of sense, which covers the sweet nut of "pure ghostliness." Were we truly spiritual, we should not need them; for our communion with Reality would then be the direct and ineffable intercourse of like with like.

Moreover, these automatisms are amongst the most dangerous instruments of self-deception. "Ofttimes," he says of those who deliberately seek for revelations, "the devil feigneth quaint sounds in their ears, quaint lights and shining in their eyes, and wonderful smells in their noses: and all is but false-hood." Hence it often happens to those who give themselves up to such experiences, that "fast after such a false feeling, cometh a false knowing in the Fiend's school: . . . for I tell thee truly, that the devil hath his contemplatives, as God hath His." Real spiritual illumination, he thinks, seldom comes by way of these psycho-sensual automatisms "into the body by the windows of our wits." It springs up within the soul in "abundance of ghostly gladness." With so great an authority it comes, bringing with it such wonder and such love, that "he that feeleth it may not have it suspect." But all other abnormal experiences—"comforts, sounds and gladness, and sweetness, that come from without suddenly"—should be set aside, as more often resulting in frenzies and feebleness of spirit than in genuine increase of "ghostly strength."

This healthy and manly view of the mystical life, as a growth towards God, a right employment of the will, rather than a short cut to hidden knowledge or supersensual experience, is one of the strongest characteristics of the writer of the *Cloud*; and constitutes perhaps his greatest claim on our respect. "Mean only God," he says again and again; "Press upon Him with longing love"; "A good will is the substance of all perfection." To those who have this good *will*, he offers his teaching: pointing out the dangers in their way, the errors of mood and of conduct into which they may fall. They are to set about this spiritual work not only with energy, but with *courtesy*: not "snatching as it were a greedy greyhound" at spiritual satisfactions, but gently and joyously pressing towards Him Whom Julian of Norwich called "our most courteous

Lord." A glad spirit of dalliance is more becoming to them than the grim determination of the fanatic.

> "Shall I, a gnat which dances in Thy ray,
> *Dare* to be reverent."

Further, he communicates to them certain "ghostly devices" by which they may overcome the inevitable difficulties encountered by beginners in contemplation: the distracting thoughts and memories which torment the self that is struggling to focus all its attention upon the spiritual sphere. The stern repression of such thoughts, however spiritual, he knows to be essential to success: even sin, once it is repented of, must be forgotten in order that Perfect Goodness may be known. The "little word God," and "the little word Love," are the only ideas which may dwell in the contemplative's mind. Anything else splits his attention, and soon proceeds by mental association to lead him further and further from the consideration of that supersensual Reality which he seeks.

The primal need of the purified soul, then, is the power of Concentration. His whole being must be set towards the Object of his craving if he is to attain to it: "Look that nothing live in thy working mind, but a naked intent stretching into God." Any thought of Him is inadequate, and for that reason defeats its own end—a doctrine, of course, directly traceable to the "Mystical Theology" of Dionysius the Areopagite. "Of God Himself can no man think," says the writer of the *Cloud*, "And therefore I would leave all that thing that I can think, and choose to my love that thing that I cannot think."

The universes which are amenable to the intellect can never satisfy the instincts of the heart.

Further, there is to be no willful choosing of method: no fussy activity of the surface-intelligence. The mystic who seeks the divine Cloud of Unknowing is to be surrendered to the direction of his deeper mind, his transcendental consciousness: that "spark of the soul" which is in touch with eternal realities. "Meddle thou not therewith, as thou wouldest help it, for dread lest thou spill all. Be thou but the tree, and let it be the wright: be thou but the house, and let it be the husbandman dwelling therein."

In the *Epistle of Privy Counsel* there is a passage which expresses with singular completeness the author's theory of this contemplative art—this silent yet ardent encounter of the soul with God. Prayer, said Mechthild of Magdeburg, brings together two lovers, God and the soul, in a narrow room where they speak much of love: and here the rules which govern that meeting are laid down by a master's hand. "When thou comest by thyself," he says, "think not before what thou shalt do after, but forsake as well good thoughts as evil thoughts, and pray not with thy mouth but list thee right well. And then if thou aught shalt say, look not how much nor how little that it be, nor weigh not what it is nor what it bemeaneth . . . and look that nothing live in thy working mind but a naked intent stretching into God, not clothed in any special thought of God in Himself. . . . This naked intent freely fastened and grounded in very belief shall be nought else to thy thought and to thy feeling but a naked thought and a blind feeling of thine own being: as if thou saidest thus unto God, within in thy meaning, 'That what I am, Lord, I offer unto Thee, without any looking to any quality of Thy Being, but only that Thou art as Thou art, without any more.' That meek darkness be thy mirror, and thy whole remembrance. Think no further of thyself than I bid thee do of thy God, so that thou be one with Him in spirit, as thus without departing and scattering, for He is thy being, and in Him thou art that thou art; not only by cause and by being, but also, He is in thee both thy cause and thy being. And therefore think on God in this work as thou dost on thyself, and on thyself as thou dost on God: that He is as He is and thou art as thou art, and that thy thought be not scattered nor departed, but proved in Him that is All."

The conception of reality which underlies this profound and beautiful passage, has much in common with that found in the work of many other mystics; since it is ultimately derived from the great Neoplatonic philosophy of the contemplative life. But the writer invests it, I think, with a deeper and wider meaning than it is made to bear in the writings even of Ruysbroeck, St. Teresa, or St. John of the Cross. "For He is thy being, and in Him thou art that thou art; not only by cause and by being, but also, He is in thee both thy cause and thy being." It was a deep thinker as well as a great lover who wrote this: one who joined hands with the philosophers, as well as with the saints.

"That meek darkness be thy mirror." What is this darkness? It is the "night of the intellect" into which we are plunged when we attain to a state of consciousness which is above thought, enter on a plane of spiritual experience with which the intellect cannot deal. This is the "Divine Darkness"—the Cloud of Unknowing, or of Ignorance, "dark with excess of light"—preached by Dionysius the Areopagite, and eagerly accepted by his English interpreter. "When I say darkness, I mean a lacking of knowing . . . and for this reason it is not called a cloud of the air, but a cloud of unknowing that is betwixt thee and thy God." It is "a dark mist," he says again, "which seemeth to be between thee and the light thou aspirest to." This dimness and lostness of mind is a paradoxical proof of attainment. Reason is in the dark, because love has entered "the mysterious radiance of the Divine Dark, the inaccessible light wherein the Lord is said to dwell, and to which thought with all its struggles cannot attain."

"Lovers," said Patmore, "put out the candles and draw the curtains, when they wish to see the god and the goddess; and, in the higher communion, the night of thought is the light of perception." These statements cannot be explained: they can only be proved in the experience of the individual soul. "Whoso deserves to see and know God rests therein," says Dionysius of that darkness, "and, by the very fact that he neither sees nor knows, is truly in that which surpasses all truth and all knowledge."

"Then," says the writer of the *Cloud*—whispering as it were to the bewildered neophyte the dearest secret of his love—"*then* will He sometimes peradventure send out a beam of ghostly light, piercing this cloud of unknowing that is betwixt thee and Him; and show thee some of His privity, the which man may not, nor cannot speak."

ABOUT PARACLETE PRESS

WHO WE ARE

PARACLETE PRESS is a publisher of books, recordings, and DVDs on Christian spirituality. Our publishing represents a full expression of Christian belief and practice—from Catholic to Evangelical, from Protestant to Orthodox.

We are the publishing arm of the Community of Jesus, an ecumenical monastic community in the Benedictine tradition. As such, we are uniquely positioned in the marketplace without connection to a large corporation and with informal relationships to many branches and denominations of faith.

WHAT WE ARE DOING

BOOKS | Paraclete publishes books that show the richness and depth of what it means to be Christian. Although Benedictine spirituality is at the heart of all that we do, we publish books that reflect the Christian experience across many cultures, time periods, and houses of worship. We publish books that nourish the vibrant life of the church and its people—books about spiritual practice, formation, history, ideas, and customs.

We have several different series, including the best-selling Living Library, Paraclete Essentials, and Paraclete Giants series of classic texts in contemporary English; A Voice from the Monastery—men and women monastics writing about living a spiritual life today; award-winning literary faith fiction and poetry; and the Active Prayer Series that brings creativity and liveliness to any life of prayer.

RECORDINGS | From Gregorian chant to contemporary American choral works, our music recordings celebrate sacred choral music through the centuries. Paraclete distributes the recordings of the internationally acclaimed choir Gloriæ Dei Cantores, praised for their "rapt and fathomless spiritual intensity" by *American Record Guide,* and the Gloriæ Dei Cantores Schola, which specializes in the study and performance of Gregorian chant. Paraclete is also the exclusive North American distributor of the recordings of the Monastic Choir of St. Peter's Abbey in Solesmes, France, long considered to be a leading authority on Gregorian chant.

DVDs | Our DVDs offer spiritual help, healing, and biblical guidance for life issues: grief and loss, marriage, forgiveness, anger management, facing death, and spiritual formation.

Learn more about us at our Web site:
www.paracletepress.com, or call us toll-free at 1-800-451-5006.

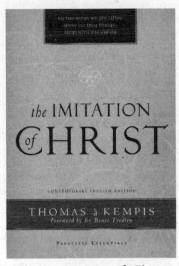

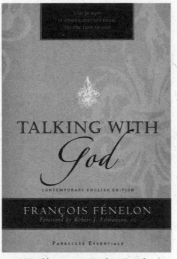

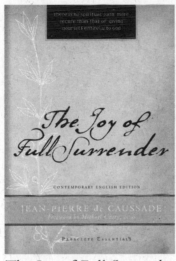

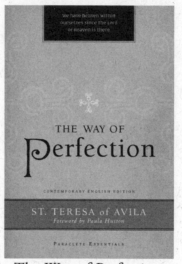